Quik Notes

*The Books of the
New Testament*

Quiknotes™
THE BOOKS OF THE NEW TESTAMENT

Philip W. Comfort, Ph.D.
Department of Biblical and Theological Studies
Wheaton College

Edited by David P. Barrett

Tyndale House Publishers, Inc.
WHEATON, ILLINOIS

Visit Tyndale's exciting Web site at www.tyndale.com

Library of Congress Cataloging-in-Publication Data

Comfort, Philip Wesley.
  Quik notes on the books of the New Testament / Philip W. Comfort ; editor,
  David P. Barrett.
      p. cm.
  Includes bibliographical references.
  ISBN 0-8423-5984-2 (pbk. : alk. paper)
  1. Bible. N.T.—Introductions. I. Barrett, David P. II. Title.
BS2330.2.C64   1999
225.6′ 1—dc20   95-40490

Printed in the United States of America

05 04 03 02 01 00 99
 7   6   5   4   3   2

TABLE OF CONTENTS

Foreword

THE NEW TESTAMENT. No other book has been so often quoted and yet so little understood. Placards are flashed at football games—"John 3:3" or "John 3:5"—yet few know what these verses actually say. The Golden Rule is quoted casually, "Do to others as you would have them do to you," but how many people know who said this and in what context? Often, the same people who say, "An eye for an eye and a tooth for a tooth" also say, "Turn the other cheek," without realizing that Jesus Christ made the second statement to counter the first.

The goal of this book is to give readers an overview of the content and context of the New Testament books. The summaries included in this work highlight major themes in each of the books and draw attention to such features as style, viewpoints, and emphases of each New Testament writer. By developing a better understanding of the content and context of each book, readers will be better equipped to grasp the larger message of the New Testament and the beliefs of the early Christian church.

Introduction

THE NEW TESTAMENT is made up of twenty-seven books written by Christians during the first century. Many of these "books" are actually letters written to churches that needed instruction or correction in their understanding and practice of Christianity. Other books, such as the four Gospels and Acts, detail the life and actions of significant figures in early Christianity. Still others, such as the book of Revelation, were written to encourage believers in their Christian faith. One feature held in common by all the books, however, is the foundational belief that Jesus Christ is the Messiah, the one sent to redeem humanity from the evil one. It is also important to note that the New Testament books were written to believers and are often difficult to understand unless they are approached from this perspective.

After the various books of the New Testament were written and began circulating among the churches, Christians collected certain books into volumes. In the first century, each of the four Gospels was treated as an individual book about Jesus' life and ministry. By the late second century, Christians had collected the four Gospels into one volume. Paul's epistles were also collected into a single volume—perhaps as early as the end of the first century. Later, in the second and third centuries, Acts and the General Epistles were combined into one volume.

In the first century, the Hebrew Bible (now called the "Old Testament" by Christians) was considered the Bible for Christians as well. They read the Old Testament and taught from it in their meetings. They also had the testimonies of the apostles who were among them. The apostles instructed the churches and passed on to them the teachings of Jesus. But after the apostles died, Christians were dependent upon what the apostles had written regarding Jesus Christ. At the same time, they began to recognize the apostles' writings as authoritative in the same way they regarded the Old Testament as Scripture. Several New Testament books were regarded as inspired Scripture as early as the second century.

Before a book could be included in the New Testament canon of Scripture, it had to measure up to a threefold standard: (1) It had to be authored by an apostle, by an associate of an apostle, or by a relative of Jesus (i.e., James or Jude); (2) it had to contain spiritual truths that could be taught as Christian doctrine; and (3) it had to be regarded by successive generations of Christians as being edifying, enlightening, and inspiring.

By the end of the first century, the New Testament canon included the four Gospels, Acts, Paul's epistles, 1 Peter, and 1 John. Other books took longer to gain acceptance into the canon of Christian writings: Hebrews (because the author was unknown), James (because it was thought to have doctrinal differences with Paul's theology on salvation), 2 Peter and Jude (because their authorship was in question), 2 and 3 John (because they were fairly unknown), and Revelation (because its message and authorship were debated). By the fourth century, most of the issues hindering canonization were resolved, and the twenty-seven books that now comprise the New Testament were recognized by the church as authoritative.

In the final arrangement of the New Testament books, the Gospels come first, recounting the life and actions of Jesus and his disciples. The early church regarded Matthew as the first Gospel to have been written, and the genealogy that opens this Gospel provides a logical link between the Old Testament and the New Testament. Mark was thought to have been written next, followed by Luke and Acts. It seemed logical to place John's Gospel among the other Gospels, and so Acts comes after John in canonical order. The letters of Paul are next, arranged according to size rather than order of composition. Likewise, the other letters that follow Paul's are arranged by size as well. Revelation appropriately concludes the New Testament with its prophetic warnings and promises of future restoration.

Historical Overview

Many of the events of the New Testament, including the life and actions of Jesus Christ, occurred in Palestine during the first century A.D. Often these events involved encounters with various religious groups or ideas that existed in Palestine during this period. In order to help today's reader understand these events in the New Testament, a brief overview of first-century Palestine has been provided.

The Law of Moses
The roots of first-century Palestinian culture stretch far back into Israelite history. The law of Moses, which is found in the first five books of the Hebrew Bible, formed the backbone of Israelite culture throughout much of their history. It provided both a social and a religious code that distinguished the Israelites from the peoples around them. While many kings rejected this code during the Divided Kingdom, nevertheless it continued to shape society. The prophets of the late Divided Kingdom railed against abuses of Mosaic law, and a massive deportation to Assyria and Babylonia was understood as a direct result of the people's failure to obey this code.

1

During this exile, a renewed concern for Mosaic law appears to have developed in order to avoid the same fate in the future. When the Israelites (also called Jews) returned from Babylonia, the temple was rebuilt, and Mosaic law was reinstated as the official social and religious code.

The Exile

The Exile had several significant effects on Jewish culture, both in Palestine and in other parts of the world. The absence of the temple in regular worship forced Judaism to develop another means for cultivating prayer, study of the Scriptures, and fellowship. The local synagogue, a small gathering place for religious purposes, fulfilled this need. Synagogues became very popular among Jews living in Palestine and throughout the world, and by the time of the first century A.D., almost every Palestinian town had one.

Aramaic, a sister language to Hebrew, also became the predominant language among the Jews. Eventually it became common practice in the synagogue for the Hebrew Scriptures to be translated into Aramaic after they were read.

After the Exile there were millions of Jews scattered throughout the world as a result of massive deportations by the Assyrians and Babylonians. Many of these Jews established synagogues and helped reshape the cultures in which they lived.

Events after the Exile

During the period of the second temple (rebuilt after the Exile), there were several significant events that shaped the culture of Palestine. The Persian Empire, which oversaw the reconstruction of Jerusalem, was eventually overthrown by Alexander the Great and his Greek empire. Alexander's empire was short-lived, however, and Palestine and Egypt came under the rule of Ptolemy I upon Alexander's death. The Ptolemies continued to rule Palestine until 198 B.C., when another Hellenistic empire, the Seleucids, gained control of Palestine.

In order to unify his vast Seleucid empire, Antiochus IV (Epiphanes) enforced a strict policy of Hellenization. This policy sought to suppress local customs and religions, so Judaism's most distinctive features, such as the Hebrew Scriptures and the rite of circumcision, came under the heaviest attack. Such persecution came to a climax when Antiochus dedicated the temple in Jerusalem to the Olympian god Zeus and sacrificed a pig (considered unclean by Jews) on the altar. These actions precipitated a revolt led by a priest named Mattathias and his sons. The revolt was successful, and the temple was retaken in 164 B.C. by Judas Maccabeus ("the hammer"). The festival of Hanukkah commemorates this event.

The Maccabean family ruled Judea until 63 B.C., when Pompey seized Palestine for the Romans. Governors directly oversaw Judea until Herod (later called "the Great") convinced the Roman senate to name him king. Herod was born an Idumean, not a Judean, and was governor of Galilee before his appointment as king of Judea. Upon Herod's death in 4 B.C., Palestine was divided up among his sons, Herod Archelaus, Herod Antipas, and Herod Philip. As each son died, his territory came under the control of Roman procurators. Herod Agrippa, grandson of Herod the Great, briefly ruled Judea from A.D. 41 to 44.

Eventually all of Palestine came under the direct control of the procurators, and the burdens they heaped upon the people became too much to bear. A massive Jewish revolt erupted in A.D. 66, but the destruction of the second temple in A.D. 70 sounded the death knell of the rebellion. The Romans quashed the final remnants of organized rebellion in A.D. 73 at the Dead Sea fortress of Masada.

Judaism after the Second Century B.C.
The dominant political and religious groups that were prevalent
in first-century Palestine had their origins in the second century
B.C. The Sadducees were a sect primarily associated with the
priesthood. They were predominantly wealthy and aristocratic.
They held only the first five books of the Hebrew Scriptures to
be authoritative, and they did not believe in angels, demons, or
the resurrection.

The sect known as the Pharisees probably arose out of a pro-
Maccabean religious group called the Hasidim, who aided in the
overthrow of the Seleucids. The Pharisees started out primarily
as a political party, but by the first century A.D. they seem to
have limited their concerns to religious matters. They were very
intent upon observing every single law given by Moses, and they
formed extensive traditions in order to ensure that Moses' laws
were carried out. The strict code of the Pharisees was comple-
mented by their insistence upon separation from those who were
more lax in their religious practices.

The Essenes, who have received an enormous amount of attention in recent years due to the discovery of the Dead Sea Scrolls,
were another religious sect who probably also arose out of the
Hasidim. The Essenes were also concerned with ritual purity, but
they were less involved in mainstream society, preferring instead
to live in separate communities and to influence others by example. The Essene community at Qumran, near the Dead Sea,
understood itself as the true Israel, and they prepared themselves
for the day when God himself would come to restore Israel.

There were also various political-activist groups, such as the
Zealots and the Sicarii, who worked for the overthrow of the
Roman government in Palestine. While it is still uncertain
whether the Zealots themselves were an actual organized group
at the time of Jesus Christ, it is clear that there were several

groups of this nature already in existence. Eventually these groups helped initiate the Jewish revolt of A.D. 66–73.

The prevailing worldview among first-century Palestinian Jews and Christians was apocalypticism. This worldview developed during the very difficult era of the Seleucid empire, when Jews were being persecuted for what they considered righteous actions. This view understood the earth as being under the control of the evil one, and the only way it would be restored was through the miraculous intervention of God himself. When this happened, the faithful righteous would be rewarded, and the evil oppressors would be judged. Various works of literature arose out of this worldview, and many of them contained similar features, including visions, riddles, supernatural encounters, and speeches about the end times and the coming of the Messiah. This worldview attempted to make theological sense of the harsh oppression that plagued Jews and Christians during these times. Most of the first-century revolts against the Romans were grounded in apocalyptic thought.

. . . . .THE LIFE AND MINISTRY OF JESUS CHRIST

Before studying the New Testament books, it is essential to become familiar with the life of Jesus Christ, since his life and actions are the touchstone for every book in the New Testament canon. The most significant, and almost sole, sources for reconstructing an outline of the life of Jesus Christ are the four Gospels of the New Testament (**Matthew, Mark, Luke,** and **John**). These four works, presented in the form of historical narrative, arrange the actions of Jesus as a definite progression from his birth to his crucifixion and resurrection. Each of the Gospels presents this progression in a unique fashion, and all four Gospels concentrate on the last three years of Jesus' life. These last three years were especially significant, since they form the period of Jesus' public ministry. Furthermore, all four Gospels devote several chapters to the last week of Jesus' life because it was in this final week that Jesus was first hailed as king, but then was betrayed, arrested, tried, and crucified. Each of the Gospels concludes with Jesus' resurrection from the dead. The Gospel of Luke adds that Jesus was then taken up into heaven.

Matthew, Mark, and Luke (the synoptic Gospels) present a fairly uniform account of Jesus' travels. According to these Gospels, Jesus journeys from Galilee to Jerusalem only once (except in Luke, where he also visits the city as a young boy). This arrangement intensifies the drama surrounding the events of Jesus' final week in Jerusalem. During this momentous last week, Jesus is first hailed as king in a triumphal entry and then is condemned to death by crucifixion. The Gospel of John, however, uses a different framework for arranging the events of Jesus' life. In this fourth Gospel, Jesus travels to Jerusalem several times, predicting from the very first visit that he would be killed by the Jewish leaders there. Thereafter, Jesus is increasingly persecuted every time he visits Jerusalem.

The following summary of the life and ministry of Jesus draws upon all four Gospels to reconstruct an outline of events. It is important to remember that the Gospel writers were not so concerned with the order of the various events as they were with the significance and meaning of each episode.

Jesus' Birth

John is the only Gospel to mention Jesus' existence before birth. John attests that Jesus existed even before the creation of the world. As the Son of God, Jesus Christ was "the Word" (the very expression of God), and he was also "God" (John 1:1). He was with God the Father from the very beginning and collaborated with him in the creation of the world (John 1:2-3). Then the Son of God became human; John describes it as "the Word became human and lived here on earth among us" (John 1:14). The beginning of John's Gospel makes it clear that he was not just recording the events of any ordinary human being; he was recounting the life and actions of the God-man himself.

Matthew and Luke provide some of the details of how Jesus' birth happened. In Matthew's account, the coming of Jesus is announced beforehand to Joseph through dreams; in Luke's account, it is announced by an angel who appears to Mary. Both Gospels are careful to point out that Jesus' birth was recognized as unique. Both Gospels affirm that Mary conceived Jesus by the Holy Spirit rather than by Joseph, to whom she was engaged. Both Gospels recall visits by strangers who also recognize Jesus' uniqueness. These visits also set the stage for the writers to emphasize the universal nature of Jesus' message.

Both Matthew and Luke link their birth accounts to genealogies. It is difficult to harmonize these genealogies since they appear to be drawn from different sources, but the purpose in both cases is to show that Jesus was legally descended from Abraham and David.

Life in Nazareth

The events of Jesus Christ's formative years are given only a few lines in the Gospels. Details are given of only one incident from his childhood: the discussion the twelve-year-old Jesus had with the religious teachers in the temple (Luke 2). This event foreshadows a key feature in Jesus' later ministry: constant debate with the Jewish religious leaders over matters of Law and Scripture. This event also presents Jesus as being acutely aware of a divine mission even at the age of twelve.

Aside from this event, not much else is said of Jesus' formative years except that he was obedient to his parents and grew in wisdom and favor. It is assumed that during his years at Nazareth Jesus learned the carpenter's trade from his adoptive father, Joseph, and became the village carpenter after Joseph's death, since he is called "the carpenter" and "the carpenter's son" in the Gospels.

The Preaching of John the Baptist

John the Baptist, the cousin of Jesus, began a national repentance movement in the wilderness sometime before Jesus' public ministry. John called the nation to be baptized as a sign of their repentance. John's methods resembled those of the Israelite prophets before the Exile. He was most likely an ascetic, since he and his followers regularly fasted, and John was described as wearing rugged clothing and eating locusts. His austere appearance and uncompromising moral challenge effectively prepared the way for the public appearance of Jesus. The importance of John's groundwork among the people can hardly be underestimated in regard to Jesus' later ministry. The Gospel writers are careful to note, however, that John was only a forerunner of Jesus. John's significance was not to eclipse the importance of Jesus and his ministry, but, rather, to set the stage for it.

The Baptism of Jesus

At age thirty, Jesus enters the public arena after his baptism by John the Baptist. All four Gospels place this event at the very beginning of Jesus' public life and emphasize the significance of this event as a divine commission. After Jesus is baptized, God declares his approval of his beloved Son, and the Holy Spirit descends upon him. This divine anointing is reminiscent of the anointing of the first several kings of Israel and Judah. Like these kings, Jesus was being divinely appointed to begin his new ministry to Israel. With his divine commission, Jesus begins his public ministry, calling the people to "turn from [their] sins and turn to God, because the Kingdom of Heaven is near."

The Temptation of Jesus

Jesus' baptism revealed the divine calling of his mission. The temptation that followed shows the nature of the environment in which he is to minister. Immediately after his baptism, Jesus is led by the Holy Spirit into the wilderness, where he fasts and is tempted by Satan. Confrontation with adverse spiritual forces characterizes Jesus' whole ministry. On this occasion, Satan confronts Jesus with the temptation to choose a path other than the one God has designed for him. In each instance, Jesus appeals to Scripture to overcome the temptation, and he refuses to take matters into his own hands. This encounter establishes from the beginning that Jesus has come to do the will of God, regardless of his own personal fate. This story also portrays Jesus as a genuine human being who, like everyone else, is subject to temptation, yet he does not yield to it.

The Early Ministry of Jesus in Judea and Samaria
Only John's Gospel tells of the work of Jesus in Judea following his baptism. In Judea Jesus calls the first disciples, John and Andrew. These first two disciples would soon be joined by three others: Peter, Philip, and Nathanael. These five formed the nucleus of the band of Jesus' followers who came to be known as the Twelve. Jesus' initial calling of these five was followed later by a more definite call to leave their occupations as fishermen in order to "fish for people" (Matthew 4; Mark 4; Luke 5).

John records that soon after Jesus began his ministry in Judea he returned to the region of Galilee, where he attended a wedding. At this wedding Jesus' mother, Mary, prompted him to turn water into wine after the wine had run out. This event is important in John's account because he notes it as the first of the signs, or miracles, that Jesus performed after leaving Judea (John 2).

Within this initial period John places two incidents that occurred at Jerusalem. The first is the cleansing of the temple (John 2:13-16). The synoptic Gospels place this event just before Jesus' trial at the end of his career, but John places it at this early stage. Angered by the money changers who were turning the temple into a marketplace instead of a house of prayer, Jesus drives them out and overturns their tables. By this display of concern for true worship, Jesus revealed the purpose of much of his ministry. The synoptic Gospels imply that this action sparked the hostility of his opponents, who would eventually kill him.

John's other incident in Jerusalem is the meeting between Jesus and Nicodemus (John 3). John uses this opportunity for Jesus to explain about being spiritually "born again" (or "born from above").

John's narrative then moves from Judea to Samaria, where Jesus encounters a Samaritan woman at a well (John 4). Pious Jews did not associate with Samaritans, since they were viewed as a mixed race and did not worship at the temple. Jesus uses the woman's physical thirst to point to her deeper spiritual thirst. Jesus then explains that he can quench this thirst because he is the one sent from God to restore true worship. The woman becomes a believer in him and spreads the news throughout Samaria.

The Period of the Galilean Ministry

After spending some time in Judea with John the Baptist, it appears that Jesus must have returned to Galilee to begin the first major phase of his ministry. Most of the information regarding Jesus' Galilean ministry is found in the synoptic Gospels. This period encompasses the events surrounding the choosing of the Twelve, the various controversies and debates with religious leaders, Jesus' miracles, and Jesus' work in northern Galilee. While the synoptic Gospels concentrate exclusively on the events in Galilee, John's account indicates that Jesus also made some visits to Jerusalem during this period.

THE CALLING OF THE DISCIPLES   In each of the synoptic Gospels there is an account of a call to four disciples to leave their fishing boats and accompany Jesus. Apparently they had already met Jesus and must have had some idea of what was involved in following him. Jesus did not appoint them at this time to be apostles, but this call was an important step toward the establishment of the twelve apostles. Another significant call came to Levi, also known as Matthew. He would certainly have been despised by his Jewish contemporaries because of his profession. But his inclusion in the special circle of Jesus' disciples shows the variety of backgrounds from which these individuals were chosen. The synoptic Gospels list the names of the twelve who eventually became apostles (Matthew 10:2-4; Mark 3:16-19; Luke 6:14-16).

The synoptic Gospels detail the instructions Jesus gave to his disciples before sending them to minister in Israel. These instructions show Jesus' concern for preparing his disciples for their future work. They were to proclaim the kingdom of God as Jesus did, but they were not to suppose that all would respond to their message. Jesus also warns them about coming hostility and persecution.

Throughout the rest of the Gospels, Jesus teaches his disciples about a wide range of topics. Most of his teaching took the form of parables; these were short stories, often about everyday events, that carried a deeper, allegorical meaning. Parables became a key feature of Jesus' ministry.

VARIOUS CONTROVERSIES AND MIRACLES   Shortly after Jesus began his public ministry, he arrived in his hometown of Nazareth and taught in the synagogue there. The people refused to believe his message, however, since he had grown up among them and was known simply as the town carpenter.

The rest of Jesus' public ministry was filled with controversies, healings, teachings, and remarkable miracles. Jesus did not hesitate to confront his contemporaries on issues involving moral or religious questions. He outraged many religious leaders by his association with the outcasts of society. Jesus often attended dinners where there were tax collectors and prostitutes, and he was willing to touch lepers and other outcasts. Through these actions, Jesus emphasized God's concern for the rejected members of society.

On several occasions, Jesus became involved in debates over the observance of the Sabbath. These controversies usually stemmed from healings that he performed on the Sabbath. Some leaders seemed to regard ritual observance of the Sabbath as of greater importance than compassionate concern for people. Jesus often deliberately performed healings to bring this issue to light. Many leaders became even more incensed because Jesus claimed that this was the work of God. Jesus' attention to the heart contrasted sharply with the widespread concern for ritual obedience.

The rising opposition to Jesus' miracles did not deter him from performing other healings. But when Jesus healed a demon-possessed man who was blind and mute, the Pharisees accused him of casting out demons by Beelzebul, the prince of the demons. Jesus argued that he was acting by the power of the Holy Spirit and that to deny this power was blasphemy. Other notable miracles were the healing of the Roman centurion's servant and the raising of a widow's dead son at Nain.

John records two visits to Jerusalem by Jesus during this period. These are difficult to date, but they probably occurred during the early period of his ministry. He attended the Feast of Tabernacles and the Feast of Dedication, or Hanukkah (John 7–10). At these times Jesus taught in the temple area and entered into dialogue with the religious leaders. The chief priests became alarmed at his presence and sent officers to arrest him. Instead of arresting him, however, John writes that the officers themselves were captivated by Jesus' teachings. More discussions with religious leaders followed. Jesus described himself as the Good Shepherd of his flock, angering many listeners, who picked up stones to kill him.

One of Jesus' miracles described by all four evangelists is the feeding of the five thousand. This event reveals Jesus' concern for the physical needs of people and marked a high point of Jesus' popularity among the people.

NORTHERN GALILEE   Jesus spent a brief time in the region of Tyre and Sidon, where he performed more healings but made it clear that his primary mission was to the people of Israel. He then moved on to Caesarea Philippi.

The discussion at Caesarea Philippi was clearly the turning point in Jesus' ministry, because it was here that Jesus asked his disciples: "Who do people say that I am?" Peter responded, "You are the Messiah, the Son of the living God." Jesus then instructed his disciples not to tell anyone the secret of his true identity.

In the synoptic Gospels, this revelation of Jesus' identity is reinforced by the Transfiguration. In the presence of Peter, James, and John, Jesus is momentarily transformed from an earthly form to a heavenly form, revealing his true nature to his disciples.

After the Transfiguration, Jesus makes two predictions concerning his approaching death. These announcements completely perplex the disciples. Peter tries to convince Jesus not to go to Jerusalem if this will be his fate, but Jesus rebukes him. Jesus is resolved to fulfill the plans of God.

The Closing Period
Luke devotes more than half his Gospel to the events between the trip to Jerusalem and Jesus' death and resurrection. In this section Luke introduces a great deal of material that is not included in the other Gospels. Parables and teachings about the kingdom of God form much of this material.

ON THE WAY TO JERUSALEM   As Jesus travels toward Jerusalem, he is aware that he will not be with the disciples much longer, and so he prepares them for the future. He teaches them about prayer, about the Father's care for them, and about his return in the future.

Along the way, Jesus visits both Jericho and Bethany. At Jericho he heals Bartimaeus and has dinner with Zacchaeus, who then reforms his crooked practices as a tax collector. Bethany was the home of Mary and Martha and their brother, Lazarus, whom Jesus had raised from the dead (John 11). It is here that Mary anoints Jesus with costly ointment. The Gospels defend her expression of love for him by noting that this anointing prepared Jesus for his burial.

JESUS' FINAL WEEK IN JERUSALEM   All four Gospels describe the Triumphal Entry of Jesus into Jerusalem. By this time many people had heard of Jesus and his miracles, and rumors were beginning to circulate that he might be the expected Messiah. While there were several different theories of what the Messiah would be like, most of them envisioned a triumphant, conquering hero who would free Israel from political oppression. This almost certainly contributed to the excitement of Jesus' grand entrance.

As Jesus rode into the city on a donkey, multitudes greeted him with praises, acclaiming him as their king. This welcome no doubt excited the disciples, who still were unclear as to Jesus' ultimate destiny.

The synoptic Gospels place the cleansing of the temple as the first main event following Jesus' entry into the city. The audacity of Jesus' actions outrages the religious leaders, and they begin to plot his demise.

Nearing his final hour, Jesus takes the opportunity to instruct his disciples about future events, especially concerning the end of the world. He reiterates the certainty of his return and mentions various signs that will precede his coming (Matthew 24; Mark 13; Luke 21). Jesus challenges the disciples to be watchful and diligent.

On the evening before Jesus was crucified, he arranged to celebrate the Passover with his disciples. The Passover meal celebrated the Israelites' deliverance from oppression in Egypt, and there were several symbolic pieces of food to be eaten and cups of wine to be drunk. As Jesus celebrated this meal with his disciples, he wished to give them a means by which the significance of his approaching death could be remembered. So he modified the ritual meal to be done in remembrance of him. Bread came to symbolize his body, and wine represented his blood, which would be poured out to seal a new covenant with his followers. This has since been called the Lord's Supper, or Holy Communion, or the Eucharist, which is still celebrated by Christians in remembrance of Jesus' death.

John's Gospel also records the story of Jesus' washing the feet of his disciples as an example of humility (John 13). He impresses upon them the importance of serving others in humility. Jesus then follows this display of humility with a series of teachings. It is here that Jesus promises to send the Holy Spirit, who will come to them after Jesus has gone.

JESUS' BETRAYAL AND ARREST   There is a sense in which the whole gospel story has been working up to a climax of rejection. The various outbursts of popular support are over, and Jesus' opposition is determined to eliminate the threat that he poses to their established system. John's Gospel refers to this approaching climax as "his hour" (John 13:1).

From the upper room, where the Last Supper was eaten, Jesus and his disciples went straight to Gethsemane, where he prayed to his Father with deep intensity and agony. He prayed that, if it was possible, he might be delivered from the suffering that awaited him. Nevertheless, he continued to submit to the Father's will. The three disciples with him fell asleep, while Judas Iscariot led a band of soldiers into Gethsemane to arrest Jesus. Judas was also one of the Twelve, but he betrayed his master for the price of a slave. Greeting him with a kiss, Judas disclosed Jesus' identity to the soldiers, and they immediately came forward to arrest him. After a brief discussion, Jesus was taken into custody while the disciples fled.

JESUS' TRIAL   There appears to have been a great deal of confusion about who held jurisdiction over Jesus' trial, and he was shuffled from place to place. The leaders questioned him about various aspects of his teaching until, finally, they settled on the charge of blasphemy for claiming to be the Messiah. Meanwhile, Peter and another disciple watched from a distance, never allowing themselves to be associated with Jesus. Peter even directly denied his connection with Jesus three times.

Eventually Jesus was handed over to Pilate, the Roman governor of Judea. Pilate appears to have been reluctant to charge Jesus with anything, since this seemed to him to be a religious dispute. The Jewish leaders pressed him, however, and charged that Jesus claimed to be a king. Pilate finally acquiesced to their demands, but he washed his hands of responsibility for Jesus' death by giving the people a choice between Jesus and Barabbas, a bandit. The people chose to crucify Jesus.

JESUS' CRUCIFIXION   Jesus was led away to be crucified the morning after his trial. Crucifixion was a standard method of execution throughout the Roman Empire. Jesus was taken to a place called "Skull Hill" outside Jerusalem. The synoptic Gospels note that a man from northern Africa named Simon was forced to carry Jesus' cross. After Jesus' hands and feet were nailed to the cross, a sign detailing the charges against him was placed above him, and he was put on display for all passersby to witness. His charges read, "This is the King of the Jews." Two bandits were also crucified with him.

Though the torturous process of crucifixion normally lasted several days for a victim, Jesus died within a few hours. John notes that as the soldiers came by to break the legs of the victims, thereby speeding up the execution, they noticed that Jesus had already died, and so they thrust a spear into his side to make certain that he was dead.

The Gospels are careful to recount Jesus' crucifixion as a fulfillment of Scripture. Many of the events surrounding Jesus' crucifixion were matched with corresponding Old Testament passages in order to show believers that this was all part of God's plan from the very beginning. A few examples include: the disciples' desertion of Jesus (Matthew 26:31 from Zechariah 13:7), the casting of lots for Jesus' tunic (John 19:24 from Psalm 22:18), and the soldiers' decision to refrain from breaking Jesus' legs (John 19:36 from Psalm 34:20).

Jesus' Burial, Resurrection, and Ascension
Jesus' body was placed in a newly hewn tomb that belonged to Joseph of Arimathea. Jesus' mother and Mary Magdalene watched as a large stone was placed over the opening to the tomb. Roman guards were stationed at the tomb to ensure that no one came to steal the body away.

On the third day after Jesus' crucifixion, Jesus was raised from the dead by the power of the Holy Spirit. The Gospels tell of an angel who came down from heaven and rolled back the stone. The guards became terrified and passed out. When Jesus' mother and Mary Magdalene came to finish preparing the body with spices, they found the tomb empty. They went back and told the disciples, who were in hiding. The disciples did not believe the women at first, but then they went and saw for themselves that the body was not in the tomb.

Later Jesus appeared to the disciples, assuring them of his resurrection and their hope. Many of these appearances occurred in Galilee, where the disciples returned after Jesus' death. Jesus then promised that he would send the Holy Spirit, and he commissioned the disciples to go throughout the whole world, making followers of Jesus Christ.

Luke adds that after forty days Jesus was then taken up into heaven, where he was seated at the right hand of God. This means that Jesus has been given the highest position of authority under God.

. . . . .THE BIRTH AND SPREAD OF THE CHRISTIAN CHURCH

The only New Testament work documenting the birth and spread of the church is the book of **Acts**. This book is a continuation of Luke's Gospel, and so the primary emphases of these two books are very similar.

The Coming of the Holy Spirit at Pentecost

Before Jesus ascended to heaven, he instructed his disciples (now called apostles) to wait until the Holy Spirit descended upon them, and then they would preach the Good News of the Resurrection throughout the earth. In the meantime they chose another disciple, Matthias, to replace Judas Iscariot, who had committed suicide after betraying Jesus.

The Jewish festival of weeks, or Pentecost, was held fifty days after Passover, and many Jews from throughout the Roman Empire had come to Jerusalem to celebrate. It was during this time that the Holy Spirit descended upon the apostles. As the apostles were filled with the Holy Spirit, they began speaking in various languages. Peter then stood up in front of a large crowd and began to preach that Jesus was the Messiah and that God had raised him from the dead. Nearly three thousand people responded to Peter's message, and they committed themselves to the apostles' teaching, to fellowship with other believers, and to the observance of the Lord's Supper. The first believers formed a sort of voluntary commune in which members sold their possessions and distributed the proceeds among the other members according to their needs. This marked the birth of the Christian church.

The Early Work of the Apostles

For the first several years, the Christian church had the immense task of defining itself and its structure. The twelve apostles oversaw much of this early work and helped establish the foundation upon which the church would be built.

Many early Christians did not completely break from Jewish religious practices. Acts 2:46 mentions that the believers met often in the temple. Throughout the first century, many Christians still attended the synagogue as well as the church. The book of James even uses the Greek word for *synagogue* rather than *church* as the place where believers would come together.

The earliest churches were located in Palestine. Likewise, the earliest converts to Christianity were Jews. Eventually, however, the gospel (Good News) of Jesus Christ would be extended to the entire Gentile world, predominantly through the work of Paul of Tarsus.

The Life and Ministry of the Apostle Paul

Paul of Tarsus is perhaps the most significant figure in the expansion of the church into the Gentile world. Highly educated in both Greek and Hebrew literature and zealous for preserving his Jewish faith, Paul (also called Saul) first entered Christian history as a persecutor of Christians. After a conversion experience on the road to Damascus, however, he became a driving force in the spread of Christianity, especially among the Gentiles. His letters to various churches form a significant portion of the New Testament corpus. The following summarizes the life and ministry of this influential apostle.

PAUL'S BACKGROUND   Paul was born in Tarsus of Cilicia (Asia Minor) to a family of Pharisees from the tribe of Benjamin (Philippians 3:5). His parents named him Saul after the first king of Israel, who was also a Benjamite, but Acts 13:9 notes that he was "also known as Paul." After Saul's conversion to Christianity in Acts, he is always referred to as "Paul," and this is the name he used in all his letters to the churches.

Paul's native city of Tarsus was a center of commerce and learning that embraced Hellenistic thinking and Roman politics. It served as the capital of the Roman province of Cilicia. In 171 B.C. Jews were brought to Tarsus to promote business in the region. It is possible that Paul's ancestors arrived in Tarsus at this time and were granted Roman citizenship. Paul inherited Roman citizenship from his father, and this proved invaluable in his travels with the gospel. Paul may have had several brothers and sisters, although only one sister is ever mentioned in the New Testament (Acts 23:16).

Paul was educated in the Law and the Prophets and became well versed in Hebrew, Aramaic, Greek, and probably Latin as well. Although born in the city of Tarsus, Paul apparently spent his youth in Jerusalem under the training of Gamaliel (Acts 22:3). It is not clear when Paul was first brought to Jerusalem, but it is likely he began his formal rabbinical studies sometime after he turned thirteen. His teacher, Gamaliel, was the grandson of Hillel, who founded a very influential Pharisaic school. Hillel's teachings can be found throughout the Talmud. Gamaliel once persuaded the Sanhedrin to spare the lives of Peter and the apostles (Acts 5:33-40). It was almost certainly during this period of study that Paul began to advance in Judaism beyond many Jews of his own age and became extremely zealous for the traditions of Judaism (Galatians 1:14). Paul eventually became a tentmaker (Acts 18:3), or perhaps a leather worker. He may have learned this trade from his father, or he may have selected it as a means of self-support, as did many in rabbinical training.

THE PERSECUTOR   While Paul was studying Jewish law in Jerusalem, Jesus was probably working as a carpenter in Nazareth. Years later, Jesus entered into public ministry and gathered together his disciples, who would one day be Paul's fellow workers in the gospel. In the meantime, however, Paul rose to a level of significant influence among the religious leaders in Jerusalem.

The sudden explosion of Christianity among Jews alarmed religious leaders in Jerusalem. Tensions increased between the new followers of Jesus and the other Jewish leaders. In time the situation came to a climax when Stephen, a follower of Jesus, angered members of a synagogue in Jerusalem (Acts 6:9-10). They accused him of blasphemy before the Sanhedrin. After Stephen's lengthy and eloquent defense, they dragged him out of the city, where he was stoned to death. The killing of this first martyr launched a wave of persecution against the followers of Jesus, and Paul was given special orders to hunt them down and arrest them.

CONVERSION AND CALLING   Paul obtained letters from the high priest to arrest believers in the Damascan synagogues and bring them to Jerusalem for trial (Acts 9:1-2). As Paul traveled to Damascus, however, he had an encounter that would forever change his life. At the outskirts of the city a light from heaven, brighter than the midday sun, shone around Paul and his entourage. Everyone fell to the ground, and Paul heard the voice of Jesus confront him and instruct him to go into the city to await further instructions. Temporarily blinded, Paul was led into Damascus, where a disciple named Ananias prayed over him.

Paul received his sight again and became a follower of Jesus as well. The Christian community forgave Paul for persecuting the church, baptized him, and helped him through the bewildering event of his conversion (Acts 9:10-22).

After a short time with the church in Damascus, Paul received death threats from Jews to whom he preached the message of Jesus, but he was protected by the believers and escaped.

PREPARATION   After Paul's experiences in Damascus, he began a several-year period of preparation, much of which was spent in the desert of Arabia. Following this, Paul returned to Damascus and then visited the apostle Peter in Jerusalem for fifteen days (Galatians 1:17-18).

At first the disciples in Jerusalem were afraid of Paul, uncertain whether he was truly a disciple of Jesus (Acts 9:26). After he was endorsed by a leader named Barnabas, however, he was accepted by the believers in Jerusalem. Paul preached in Jerusalem, but when his life was threatened once again, the believers sent him away to Tarsus (Acts 9:29-30; Galatians 1:21).

The end of Paul's preparation came when Barnabas went to Tarsus to look for him and to bring him to Antioch (Acts 11:25-26). By this time Paul had been living in Cilicia for ten years, boldly proclaiming the message of Jesus.

SENT OUT FROM ANTIOCH   The church in Antioch was formed by believers who fled persecution in Jerusalem after the death of Stephen (Acts 11:19). At first the scattered believers shared the gospel only with Jews. In Antioch, however, the gospel was opened to the Gentiles as well, and many became believers. It is fitting that Paul, the apostle to the Gentiles (Acts 22:21; Romans 11:13), should appear in Antioch to formally begin his ministry.

Barnabas and Paul stayed with the church in Antioch for a year. It was here that the new name *Christian* was coined to distinguish the followers of Jesus from other Gentiles and Jews (Acts 11:26). Hearing of a famine in Judea, the Christians in Antioch determined to send relief to the believers in Judea. Barnabas and Paul delivered the church's gift, and the potency of the gospel among the Gentiles was clearly displayed to the Jewish churches. Afterward, Barnabas and Paul returned to Antioch with John Mark, Barnabas's cousin.

Beginning from the Day of Pentecost, the work in the gospel had been fairly incidental. Contacts were made in homes, the marketplace, the streets, synagogues, highways, etc. But in Antioch, a determined effort was made to evangelize a specific section of the Roman Empire (Acts 13:1-3). The church designated Barnabas and Paul for this work. With the prayers and encouragement of the church and with John Mark as their assistant, Barnabas and Paul set sail for Cyprus.

TRAVEL WITH BARNABAS   Arriving in Salamis, Paul and Barnabas traveled the length of the island of Cyprus, preaching in synagogues along the way (Acts 13:5-6). When they reached Paphos, the Roman proconsul, Sergius Paulus, wanted to hear the word of God. A magician named Elymas Bar-Jesus tried to prevent the proconsul from believing but was stricken with temporary blindness at Paul's command.

Paul and his companions then set sail from Paphos and arrived in Perga of Pamphylia. John Mark deserted them there and returned to his home in Jerusalem (Acts 13:13). This apparently caused some dissension between Paul, Barnabas, and John Mark, but Paul and Mark were later reconciled (Colossians 4:10; 2 Timothy 4:11).

Paul's travels with the gospel continued throughout the mainland of Asia Minor, specifically in the Roman provinces of Galatia, Pamphylia, Pisidia, and Lycaonia. Paul and Barnabas were asked to speak at the synagogue of Antioch in Pisidia (Acts

13:15). After they delivered their message, they were invited to speak the next week. Acts records that "almost the entire city turned out to hear them preach the word of the Lord" (Acts 13:44). The jealousy that was stirred up among Jews who opposed Paul's message precipitated his decisive turn to the Gentiles. Many Gentiles in Antioch believed the gospel and spread it throughout the region, but Paul and Barnabas were forced out and went to Iconium in Lycaonia (Acts 13:48-51).

Paul and Barnabas experienced the same success and opposition in Iconium that they had in Antioch (Acts 14:1), and the apostles fled the threat of a stoning. In Lystra Paul healed a man who had been crippled since birth (Acts 14:8-10). The citizens began worshiping Paul and Barnabas as the Roman gods Mercury and Jupiter, who were believed to have visited this region. Paul had to convince the people that he and Barnabas were merely mortals who served the living God.

It was in Lystra that Paul received his first serious persecution for the gospel. Many Jews there stoned him, dragged him out of the city, and left him for dead (Acts 14:19). Paul's disciples came to his aid, Paul recovered, and then he moved on to Derbe with Barnabas. After making many disciples in Derbe, the apostles retraced their steps through Lystra, Iconium, and Pisidian Antioch, strengthening and encouraging the new believers and appointing elders in each church (Acts 14:21-23). Arriving again in Perga, they sailed back to Syrian Antioch, where they reported to the church the news that God had extended the gospel to the Gentiles.

THE COUNCIL OF JERUSALEM   In Syrian Antioch, many Jews opposed Paul's message of grace, which did not require Gentiles to keep the law of Moses. These Jews began teaching the Christians there that they must be circumcised according to Mosaic law. This caused a heated debate between Paul and the Jewish leaders. It is very possible that Paul's letter to the **Galatians** may have been written around this time (ca. A.D. 49), although some scholars date this letter later (ca. A.D. 56). Paul wrote this bold letter to counteract the legalistic influence of many Jews in Galatia and to show that the grace provided by Jesus Christ was sufficient and could be obtained by faith alone. The epistle of **James** was probably written around this time as well. While it is debated whether this letter from Jesus' brother is actually antithetical to Paul's letter to the Galatians, it is clear that it represents a very Jewish perspective regarding Christianity.

In order to settle the controversy regarding Mosaic law, the church in Antioch sent Paul, Barnabas, and others to Jerusalem to meet with the apostles and elders there (Acts 15:2). Along the way they spread the news of Gentile conversions. This brought great joy to the believers, but such joy was not shared by some in Jerusalem. In the first meeting of the Jerusalem Council, some argued that the Gentiles should be "required to follow the law of Moses" (Acts 15:5). Peter countered this by insisting that "we are all saved the same way, by the special favor of the Lord Jesus" (Acts 15:11). After long debate, James, the brother of Jesus, reached the decision that they should not trouble those Gentiles who were turning to God (Acts 15:19). A few basic restrictions were placed upon the Gentile believers, but the Mosaic law, as a whole, was not enforced. An official letter was drawn up to be sent to the churches, informing them of the decision. This was a significant decision for the Christian church, and the news was received joyfully by the church in Antioch.

FURTHER TRAVEL   Paul desired to revisit the churches that he and Barnabas had visited earlier. He wanted to see how they were doing (Acts 15:36). Barnabas wanted to take John Mark with them, but Paul refused since John Mark had deserted them during their earlier journey (Acts 13:13). A sharp disagreement over this matter ended Barnabas's association with Paul. Silas, a leader among the brothers in Jerusalem, accompanied Paul as he set out by land through Syria and Cilicia, strengthening the churches there (Acts 15:40-41).

Beginning from Derbe in Galatia, Paul and Silas revisited the churches that Paul had helped establish earlier. While in Lystra they were joined by Timothy (Acts 16:1-3). The apostles delivered the letter from the Jerusalem Council to these young churches.

It is likely that Ephesus, a major city in the Roman province of Asia, was Paul's primary objective for advancing the gospel, but he was told by the Holy Spirit not to speak the word in Asia (Acts 16:6). They attempted to turn north and enter the region of Bithynia, "but again the Spirit of Jesus did not let them go" (Acts 16:7). So Paul and his party were forced to continue straight westward to Troas, on the Aegean Sea, where Luke probably joined them. After experiencing a vision in which he was called out of Asia into Macedonia (Acts 16:8-9), Paul and his party immediately crossed by boat into Europe, where they carried the gospel to Philippi, Thessalonica, Berea, Athens, and Corinth.

Philippi was a Roman colony and military outpost where there were few Jews, so Paul went to a place by the river where the local Jews gathered to pray. He spoke to some women there, notably Lydia, who believed and was baptized, along with her whole household (Acts 16:12-15). Paul also cast a spirit of divination out of a girl there, and, as a result, he and Silas were arrested, flogged, and jailed (Acts 16:16-24). Paul eventually disclosed his Roman citizenship and was released, but he was asked to leave the city. From Philippi, Paul traveled to Thessalonica.

Some Jews at Thessalonica became jealous of Paul's success in communicating the gospel, and they gathered a mob to search for the apostles. They complained to the city authorities that the men who had "turned the rest of the world upside down" had come to disturb their city, and they accused the apostles of professing "allegiance to another king [besides Caesar], Jesus" (Acts 17:5-7).

Paul and Silas quickly left Thessalonica by night and arrived in Berea, whose citizens eagerly and thoughtfully received the gospel (Acts 17:10-12). Some Thessalonian Jews, however, had followed Paul to Berea to incite the crowds. The believers then sent Paul away to Athens, while Silas and Timothy stayed behind.

The Athenians quickly labeled Paul a babbler but let him air his views before the Areopagus. Paul's speech there displayed a broad knowledge of Greco-Roman philosophy, poetry, sculpture, architecture, and religion. He made reference to an altar to "an Unknown God," but his speech was cut short when he mentioned the Resurrection (Acts 17:22-32). Paul's words delighted the minds of many but influenced the wills of few. When he arrived in Corinth, Paul determined not to proclaim the mystery of God in lofty or wise words, so that the believers' faith would not rest on human wisdom but on the power of God (1 Corinthians 2:1-5).

In Corinth Paul met Aquila and Priscilla (or Prisca), Roman Jews with whom he lived and worked as a tentmaker. Eventually these two would become prominent among the churches (Romans 16:3; 1 Corinthians 16:19; 2 Timothy 4:19). Paul stayed in Corinth eighteen months in A.D. 50–51, establishing and strengthening the church there. It was most likely during this time that Paul wrote two letters (**1 and 2 Thessalonians**) to the church in Thessalonica, encouraging them to lead holy, industrious lives in the hope of the second coming of Jesus Christ.

Accompanied by Priscilla and Aquila, Paul set sail from Corinth to Syria. Along the way he stopped at Ephesus, leaving Priscilla and Aquila there as he then sailed on to Caesarea. After briefly visiting Jerusalem, Paul returned to Antioch, where he remained for a while (Acts 18:18-23). He departed alone from Antioch, going from place to place in Galatia and Phrygia and strengthening the disciples. Eventually he arrived back in Ephesus (Acts 18:23; 19:1).

LABOR IN THE GOSPEL   At Ephesus a man from Alexandria named Apollos had been preaching eloquently about "the way of the Lord," though he had only been made a disciple of John the Baptist. Priscilla and Aquila took him aside and explained more fully who Jesus was. After that he began to preach that Jesus was the Messiah. Paul also instructed some disciples of John the Baptist (Acts 19:1-7), explaining to them the significance of Jesus and the work of the Holy Spirit. He then spent three months preaching at the local synagogue until members of the congregation "spoke against the Way."

Paul led John's disciples to the neutral ground of Tyrannus's school (Acts 19:9), where Jews and Greeks were free to come. He continued his work there for two years, and "people throughout the province of Asia—both Jews and Greeks—heard the Lord's message" (Acts 19:10).

In Ephesus Paul enjoyed an effective ministry bolstered by extraordinary miracles, a public burning of sorcery books, and the assistance from officials of the province of Asia (Acts 19:11-41). But there were many adversaries, especially among the artisans associated with the temple of Diana. Paul's ministry had hurt their trade to the extent that they incited a riot (Acts 19:23-41). Paul had intended to stay in Ephesus until Pentecost (1 Corinthians 16:8), but this tumult seems to have hastened his departure.

During Paul's stay in Ephesus, someone from Corinth sent word that there were divisions in the Corinthian church (1 Corinthians 1:10-13). This report generated a flurry of letters and travels. Paul wrote a letter to Corinth, but this letter is now lost, unless it is part of 2 Corinthians (1 Corinthians 5:9). The church in Corinth wrote back (1 Corinthians 7:1) and sent messengers to

Paul (1 Corinthians 16:17). Paul sent Timothy to them (1 Corinthians 4:17; 16:10). Paul then wrote what is now known as **1 Corinthians** around A.D. 53 and sent it by Titus, who was to meet him in Troas to report the results (2 Corinthians 2:12-13).

After his hurried exit from Ephesus, Paul found an open door for the gospel in Troas, but he so longed to hear from Corinth that he pushed on into Macedonia (2 Corinthians 2:12-13). There he was finally comforted by news from Titus (2 Corinthians 7:5-7) and rejoiced over the Corinthians' repentance and renewed enthusiasm (2 Corinthians 7:8-16). From Macedonia Paul wrote what is now known as **2 Corinthians** (A.D. 54), toured northwest to proclaim the Good News of Christ in Illyricum (Romans 15:19), and then turned south for Achaia and his third visit to Corinth (Acts 19:21; 20:1-3; 2 Corinthians 13:1).

During a three-month winter stay in Corinth (A.D. 55–56), Paul wrote the letter to the **Romans,** which solidified his explanation of the gospel. Paul had many personal friends in Rome (Romans 16) and had long intended to visit there (Romans 1:9-15). But first he wanted to deliver relief funds from the Gentile churches to the Jerusalem church (Romans 15:25-26; 1 Corinthians 16:1). He then planned to visit Rome on his way to Spain.

THE ARREST IN JERUSALEM   As Paul traveled from Corinth, he was repeatedly warned of danger awaiting him in Jerusalem, but he insisted on continuing. He carried the collection for Jerusalem, journeying swiftly in order to reach Jerusalem by Pentecost (Acts 20:16). They proceeded by land from Achaia, through Macedonia, and on to Philippi in time for Passover (spring A.D. 56). Crossing by sea to Troas, they visited the believers there and then sailed to Miletus through the archipelago of the eastern Aegean Sea (Acts 20:7-16). From Miletus Paul sent for the elders of Ephesus and passionately warned them of false teachers who would soon come (Acts 20:17-38).

Paul and his companions then set sail to Cos, to Rhodes, and then to Patara, where they changed ships for Phoenicia (Acts 21:1-2). A straight course to Tyre brought them within sight of Cyprus (Acts 21:3). The disciples in Tyre again warned Paul not to go on to Jerusalem, but he pressed on to Caesarea, where he and his company stayed with Philip, who had formerly served with the martyred Stephen. In Caesarea, Paul still would not be persuaded by an especially dramatic prophecy of his coming arrest (Acts 21:10-14).

In Jerusalem Paul's entourage stayed with Mnason and were warmly welcomed by the other Christians there (Acts 21:15-17). James and the church elders praised God when they heard what had been accomplished among the Gentiles (Acts 21:18-20). They thankfully received the collection from the churches but warned Paul of his bad reputation among the thousands of Jewish Christians in Jerusalem. They urged him to convince the believers that he did not encourage forsaking the Mosaic customs (Acts 21:20-24). In order to correct this misunderstanding, Paul agreed to join in a sacred Jewish vow ceremony.

While Paul's vow may have satisfied the Christians, there were still many Jews who despised him. Jews from Asia, visiting Jerusalem for the Pentecost feast (A.D. 57), incited a riot against Paul (Acts 21:27-29), and the whole city became involved. The crowd dragged Paul out of the temple and tried to kill him, but he was rescued by Roman soldiers. Paul made a futile attempt to explain himself to the crowd, and the soldiers brought him into the barracks. The soldiers prepared to flog Paul, but at the last minute he revealed his inherited Roman citizenship. At this the Roman tribune became afraid to deal with Paul until he had learned more of the charges against him (Acts 22:25-30).

Paul was brought before a council of Jewish leaders. He began his defense with heated words but changed his strategy when he noticed many Pharisees at the council. He intentionally created bitter dissension between the council members by insisting that he was being tried for belief in the resurrection of the dead. The uproar between the Pharisees and the Sadducees over this issue caused the tribune to take Paul back into the barracks. There the Lord appeared to him and encouraged him, promising that he would present his defense in Rome (Acts 23:10-11).

In the meantime, more than forty Jews vowed not to eat or drink until they had killed Paul (Acts 23:12-15). With the help of Paul's nephew, however, the conspiracy was exposed. For safety, Paul was taken from Jerusalem to Caesarea under guard of 470 soldiers and handed over to the custody of Felix, the governor (Acts 23:16-35). Over a period of two years in Caesarea, Paul was brought before Felix; his successor, Festus; and King Agrippa. Festus suggested that Paul be returned to Jerusalem for trial, but Paul knew the murderous intent of his accusers and appealed his case to Caesar himself (Acts 25:9-12).

VOYAGE AND STAY IN ROME   In order to plead his case before Caesar, Paul and his companions, Aristarchus and Luke, were taken to Rome by way of a perilous sea voyage (A.D. 58, Acts 27:1–28:16). Luke's account of the journey from Caesarea to Rome is a treasure of information on ancient ships, navigation, and seamanship. Luke traces the voyage stage by stage through every crisis, with a change of ship at Myra, a delay at Fair Havens on Crete, and a shipwreck on Malta.

In the spring of A.D. 59, they arrived at Puteoli, Italy, and made their way to Rome, welcomed by believers along the Appian Way (Acts 28:13-15). Paul was allowed to live in a house of his own under Roman guard (Acts 28:16, 30). There he received the local Jewish leaders and taught about Jesus without interference. Paul most likely penned several letters to churches during this period (A.D. 60–62), including those known as the Prison Epistles. Paul's letter to the **Ephesians** (though it was most likely sent to each of the Asian churches) was probably the first. This epistle discusses the great mystery of Christ and the church. The second and third epistles were sent to the **Colossians** and **Philemon**. The personal letter to Philemon was sent along with the letter to the Colossian church, since Philemon was a member there. The letter to the Colossians asserts the superiority of Christ over all other religions and philosophies, while the letter to Philemon is Paul's appeal on behalf of a runaway slave named Onesimus. The letter to the **Philippians** was sent last, expressing Paul's aspirations to know Christ and anticipating release from prison.

FINAL YEARS AND MARTYRDOM   Apparently Paul made quite an impression on the Roman guard in his home, and several members of Caesar's household became believers—perhaps through Paul's ministry (Philippians 4:22). It is possible that a good report about Paul was given to Caesar as a result, and Paul was released from prison around A.D. 62. Romans 15:28 indicates that Paul intended to visit Rome on his way to Spain after he delivered the collection to Jerusalem. His arrest and imprisonment in Jerusalem altered these plans. Paul may still have gone to Spain after his release, which came a couple years before the burning of Rome on July 19, A.D. 64. Returning east, Paul left Titus in Crete (Titus 1:5) and traveled through Miletus, south of Ephesus, where he left Trophimus (2 Timothy 4:20). Traveling toward Macedonia, Paul visited Timothy in Ephesus (1 Timothy 1:3). Along the way Paul left his cloak and books with Carpus in Troas (2 Timothy 4:13). He may have intended to return there later for his possessions.

From Macedonia Paul wrote **1 Timothy,** a loving letter of instruction to his young coworker in the gospel (A.D. 63–64). Paul decided to spend the winter in Nicopolis (Titus 3:12), northwest of Corinth on the Adriatic Sea, but was still in Macedonia when he wrote to **Titus**. This letter is similar to 1 Timothy, yet with a somewhat harsher tone. This letter also gives a final glimpse of the eloquent and zealous Apollos (Titus 3:13), who is still in association with Paul ten or more years after his first appearance in Ephesus (Acts 18:24).

From here Paul's path is obscure. He may have wintered in Nicopolis, but he did not return to Troas for his winter cloak (2 Timothy 4:13). At some point he was arrested by the Romans, because he spent a winter in Rome's Mamertine Prison, suffering from the cold in a rock cell. Paul may have been anticipating the coming winter when he requested that Timothy bring his cloak (2 Timothy 4:13, 21). During this imprisonment Paul wrote **2 Timothy** (A.D. 66–67). Paul wrote this letter because he was anxious to see his disciple before his own death. In case Timothy did not arrive in time, however, Paul felt it necessary to warn him of the heresies that were infecting the churches.

While it is possible that the charges against Paul were related to the burning of Rome, it is not certain. By this time it was "illegal" to be a Christian, since it was no longer protected by Roman law as a sect of Judaism. These circumstances made life very dangerous for Paul at this time. Many of his workers deserted him (2 Timothy 4:16), including all the Christians who had come from Asia (2 Timothy 1:15) and Demas (2 Timothy 4:10). Only Luke, the author of Luke and Acts, was with him when he wrote his second letter to Timothy (2 Timothy 4:11). Faithful believers still in hiding in Rome were also in contact with the apostle (2 Timothy 1:16; 4:19, 21). Paul instructed Timothy to come to him in Rome and to bring Mark with him (2 Timothy 4:11). Apparently Timothy did come and was imprisoned (Hebrews 13:23). Paul's request for the books and parchments (2 Timothy 4:13) discloses that he was reading and studying to the end.

The apostle Paul had two hearings before Emperor Nero. At his first defense, Paul not only pleaded his own cause but also that of the gospel, still longing that all the Gentiles would hear its message (2 Timothy 4:17). Perhaps no decision was made, and thus he was rescued from "certain death" (2 Timothy 4:17). Though he knew he would soon die, Paul was not afraid; he was assured that the Lord would reward him at the end of time (2 Timothy 4:8). Finally, the apostle blessed all believers: "May the Lord be with your spirit. Grace be with you all" (2 Timothy 4:22). After this, the New Testament is silent regarding Paul.

Nothing is known of Paul's second hearing except that it resulted in the sentence of capital punishment. The events surrounding Paul's death are unrecorded. Nero died in the summer of A.D. 68, so Paul was probably executed before that date. As a Roman citizen, Paul must have been spared the torture that often attended such a sentence. Tradition holds that Paul was decapitated by the sword of an imperial headsman on the Ostian Road just outside of Rome and was buried nearby. This fulfilled Paul's desire "to go and be with Christ" (Philippians 1:23).

Later Work of the Apostles

The other apostles continued to spread the gospel throughout the Roman Empire after Paul's death. Peter apparently established a ministry in Rome, where he wrote **1 Peter** (ca. A.D. 63). This letter was written to several churches throughout Asia to console those who were experiencing hardship for the sake of the gospel. He encouraged them to live godly lives among unbelievers in order to present a living example of the gospel of Jesus Christ. The epistle of **2 Peter** is traditionally thought to have been written late in Peter's life. This letter warns against false teachers and encourages the readers to grow in their faith. Tradition holds that Peter was eventually martyred around A.D. 66.

The letter to the **Hebrews** was most likely written by a close associate of Paul. It is doubtful that Paul himself penned it, based upon differences in the structure and style of the book. This book was written to admonish and instruct a group of believers who were apparently having second thoughts about the superiority of Christianity over Judaism. The epistle of **Jude** was written to defend the truth against false teaching that led to complete lawlessness. It is ascribed to the brother of Jesus, who was also the brother of James.

The apostle John also carried on a significant ministry well beyond Paul's lifetime. As an elder to the church in Ephesus, John wrote **1, 2,** and **3 John** to nearby churches in Asia in order to warn them against false teaching. The Gospel of **John** was probably written some time after these letters. The book of **Revelation** is also attributed to the apostle John. This apocalyptic book draws upon imagery from the Old Testament to encourage Christians who were being persecuted for the gospel.

. . . . .CHRONOLOGY OF NEW TESTAMENT EVENTS

6/5 B.C. Birth of Jesus Christ
A.D. 6/7 Young Jesus in the Temple
A.D. 26 John the Baptist Begins His Ministry
A.D. 26/27 Jesus Christ Is Baptized, Begins His Ministry
A.D. 30 Jesus Christ Is Crucified and Resurrected
A.D. 30 Coming of the Holy Spirit at Pentecost
A.D. 34/35 Paul's Conversion
A.D. 44 James the Apostle Is Martyred
A.D. 46–48 Paul's First Missionary Journey
A.D. 49/50 Jerusalem Council
A.D. 50–52 Paul's Second Missionary Journey
A.D. 53–57 Paul's Third Missionary Journey
A.D. 60–62 Paul's Imprisonment in Rome
A.D. 67 Paul's Second Imprisonment
A.D. 65–67 Peter Martyred

A.D. 68 Paul Martyred
A.D. 90–95 John Exiled

. . . . APPROXIMATE DATES OF NEW TESTAMENT BOOKS

45–50 James
49 Galatians
50/51 1 and 2 Thessalonians
56/57 1 and 2 Corinthians
58 Romans
61 Ephesians
61 Colossians, Philemon
62 Philippians
63 1 Timothy
63 Hebrews
63 1 Peter
63 (?) Mark
64–67 (?) Luke-Acts
65 (?) Matthew
65–67 Titus
67 (?) 2 Peter
68 2 Timothy
75 (?) Jude
80–85 (?) Epistles of John
85 (?) John
90–95 Revelation

Book Summaries

, ...LETTERS OF THE NEW TESTAMENT

Most of the New Testament books are not really books at all but first-century letters (epistles). With the exception of the Gospels and Acts and possibly Hebrews and Revelation, all of the New Testament books follow the standard format of the day for personal and official correspondence.

Some of the New Testament letters were written as personal letters, beginning with (1) an identification of the writer and (2) a salutation to the recipient of the letter, followed by (3) a blessing or word of well-wishing to the recipient and perhaps a few details about the time and place of writing. After this introduction, (4) the body of the letter follows. A few (5) greetings to specific individuals usually conclude the letter, along with (6) a final benediction. Archeologists have uncovered hundreds of Hellenistic letters that follow this general format. Paul's letter to Philemon and the second and third letters of John are the best examples of personal letters in the New Testament.

Some Hellenistic writers used the letter form as a literary vehicle to present certain themes. This form allowed for a personal presentation of a weighty topic without sounding pretentious. Most of the New Testament letters follow this format. They have the same basic form as a personal letter, but their contents are not just personal exchanges—they develop substantial discourses about spiritual truths. Some of Paul's epistles could even be called treatises. Romans is a treatise on God's eternal plan for his chosen people, and Ephesians is a treatise on the great mystery of Christ and the church.

The Letters of Paul to the Churches

The letters of the apostle Paul comprise nearly one-third of the entire New Testament. These epistles are vital to the church because they establish Christian doctrine and explain Christian practice. In the following summaries, Paul's epistles are presented in chronological order in order to help the reader grasp the historical development of Paul's work and writings. The history of this development is intricately linked with the history of Paul's life and travels as presented in the book of Acts. Therefore the reader is encouraged to study each letter in conjunction with the circumstances that surrounded its composition.

GALATIANS   Paul's epistle to "the churches of Galatia" (1:2) has been called the "Magna Carta" of spiritual emancipation. Martin Luther called it "my own epistle." Through the concrete (and potentially explosive) context of real-life events, Paul resolves the dispute over justification by faith. The decision established in this epistle became the touchstone for the rest of Paul's letters.

The actual region of Galatia to which the letter refers is often debated. The official region of Galatia is a district in Asia Minor bordering on Phrygia, Pontus, Bithynia, Cappadocia, and Pamphylia. Most modern scholars consider the area mentioned in the letter to be southern Galatia, which encompassed the cities visited by Paul on his first and second missionary journeys. Other scholars define the area as northern Galatia. Likewise, the date of the letter's composition is disputed. Much of the debate hinges on a meeting at Jerusalem mentioned in Galatians 2:1-10. If this meeting is identical to the Jerusalem Council recorded in Acts 15, then Paul probably wrote this epistle around A.D. 56. If the two meetings are different, then this epistle may well have been written as early as A.D. 49, making it the first of Paul's letters.

The Galatians had received Paul's gospel message with joy at first, but they soon wavered in their allegiance to his teaching when some false teachers instructed them to observe the laws of Moses in order to please God (2:11-13). These false teachers almost convinced the Galatians to undergo circumcision, a key act of obedience to Mosaic law. They also accused Paul of falsely representing himself as a divinely commissioned apostle when, in fact, he was but a messenger sent by the apostles in Jerusalem. They added that his teaching contradicted that of Peter and James and should not be accepted.

Paul's purpose, then, in writing this epistle was (1) to defend his apostolic authority; (2) to counteract the false teachers' influence in Galatia, showing that their doctrine destroyed the very essence of Christianity; and (3) to strengthen the Galatian believers in their Christian faith. Paul had already confronted the false teachers and the Galatians face-to-face, and now he was writing to finally put an end to the whole debate.

The tone of this epistle combines the two extremes of sternness and tenderness. Paul's beginning is abrupt, reflecting the urgency of his concerns. As he develops his thoughts, however, a warmhearted tenderness can be found in Paul's admonitions. The epistle ends with a final warning against false teaching and a closing benediction.

Introduction (1:1-10)
God's Special Revelation to Paul (1:11–2:21)
Freedom through Grace Rather than the Law (3:1–4:31)
Freedom in the Spirit (5:1–6:10)
Conclusion (6:11-18)

1 THESSALONIANS   The first letter of Paul to the Thessalonians urges the believers to lead lives worthy of the kingdom that would soon be established at the return of Christ. Paul addresses this young church as a father would instruct a growing child, commending them for their strengths and admonishing them in their weaknesses.

Paul probably wrote this epistle from Corinth, where Timothy and Silas rejoined him soon after he arrived in A.D. 50. It was written not long after the church was founded at Thessalonica, as indicated by Paul's comment that he was taken from them for a short time (2:17). At the time, Thessalonica was the capital of the Roman district of Macedonia, and it enjoyed a thriving economy. The Thessalonian church had been established by Paul after his imprisonment and flogging at Philippi. The Thessalonian believers received the gospel joyfully, despite persecution from their own countrymen and from many Jews (1:6; 2:13-16). The church continued to grow, and the gospel spread from there throughout Macedonia, Achaia, and elsewhere (1:7-8). Paul eventually moved on to Athens and then to Corinth, where he wrote this epistle.

Timothy brought a good report to Paul concerning the Thessalonian church. They abounded in faith and love and longed to see Paul, just as Paul longed to see them (3:6-10). Thus they were healthy in the faith, but they also needed Paul's guidance in several matters. Apparently some among them needed to be warned against adultery (4:3-7) and revelry (5:5-8). Some may have lacked respect for their leaders (5:12-13), and others were obstructing the work of the Spirit (5:19-20). Paul corrected these believers while affirming his love for them. Some whose relatives had died needed comfort and instruction concerning whether their relatives would also be included in the kingdom, since they had died before Christ's return.

Throughout the letter Paul remains appropriately calm and equable, since he is only dealing with various practical offenses rather than significant doctrinal controversies. Overall, the letter is very encouraging and affirming of the young church.

Salutation (1:1)
Reputation of the Thessalonian Church (1:2-10)
Review of Paul's Relationship with Them (2:1–3:13)
Addressing Problems within the Church (4:1–5:11)
Conclusion (5:12-28)

2 THESSALONIANS   In his second letter to the Thessalonians, Paul encourages those who are being persecuted for the gospel and clarifies his earlier statements regarding the return of Christ. Apparently, after Paul had first written to the Thessalonians, many believers became confused about the return of Christ and misunderstood Paul's statements in the first letter. Others stirred up the church with rumors that Christ had already returned. Some professed to know by the Spirit (2:2) that this was so; others alleged that Paul had said this when he was with them. It seems that there was even a letter falsely ascribed to Paul that circulated among the believers, stirring up more confusion. Some members of the church were even neglecting their daily work, possibly in anticipation of Christ's impending return.

Paul corrects these misunderstandings of Christ's return by asserting that there must first be a time of great rebellion when "the man of lawlessness" would be revealed. When he is finally revealed, the Lord will destroy him. Paul then explains how those who refuse to obey the gospel are being deceived by this same evil power. It is difficult to know exactly what Paul is writing about, but the overall message is clear—Jesus Christ has not yet returned, and so believers must continue living their lives in obedience to the gospel. No one was to become lazy, depending entirely upon others for their food. Paul also cautions the church to look for his own signature on any letters ascribed to him, so that they are not deceived again.

It is almost certain that this second letter to the Thessalonians was written in Corinth shortly after the first letter (ca. A.D. 51). The epistle was written jointly with Timothy and Silas, who were with Paul for only a short while.

The distinguishing mark of this letter is Paul's use of apocalyptic imagery in his discussion about the return of Christ. Paul draws upon imagery resembling that of Daniel, Zechariah, and the apocalyptic passages of the Gospels (which were written later than this letter).

Salutation (1:1-2)

Thanksgiving for Their Faith, Love, and Perseverance (1:3-12)

Signs of the End Times (2:1-17)

Final Exhortations and Greetings (3:1-18)

1 CORINTHIANS The letters that are now called 1 and 2 Corinthians actually belong to an original collection of four letters to the Corinthian church. The first of these letters, which is now lost, is referred to in 1 Corinthians 5:9: "when I wrote to you before, I told you not to associate with people who indulge in sexual sin." One topic of this first letter seems to have been a contribution to be made for Christians in Jerusalem. Shortly after his first letter, however, Paul received news of various problems in the Corinthian church, so he sent a second letter, now called 1 Corinthians, to address the issues of concern.

Paul wrote 1 Corinthians from Ephesus (16:8), probably around the year A.D. 56. His allusion to Passover imagery in 5:7 suggests that he was writing around the time of Passover.

The city of Corinth was well known for its wealth and commerce, which resulted from its ideal location on the Greek peninsula. In Paul's time it was the capital of the the Greek province of Achaia and the seat of the Roman proconsul. The city was notorious for wild living—even among jaded Roman soldiers— so much so that the Greek phrase "to Corinthianize" had become a proverbial phrase for engaging in sexually immoral behavior. This climate no doubt contributed to many of the problems in the Corinthian church.

Several of the problems Paul addresses in 1 Corinthians had been communicated to him by a Corinthian church member. There were rival factions, incest among believers, public lawsuits between fellow Christians, abuses of spiritual gifts, and disorderly conduct during church meetings and the Lord's Supper. Paul addresses each of these problems, pointing to Christ as the ultimate solution.

Paul also answers questions that the Corinthians had asked in a letter (7:1). He counsels them about marriage and sexual relations, about eating food that had been offered to idols, about the use of spiritual gifts in public worship, and about the resurrection of Christ and his followers. In the end, Paul gives them instructions for the collection to be taken for needy Christians in Jerusalem (16:1).

This letter is a prime example of what has been called the *occasional* epistle. That is, while the letter contains a few themes and systematic discourses, it focuses primarily upon specific issues that need to be corrected. First Corinthians provides the Christian church with an actual sample of how specific problems were addressed and corrected in the early church.

Prologue (1:1-9)
Addressing Factions within the Church (1:10–4:21)
Addressing Moral and Ethical Problems (5:1–6:20)
Instruction about Marriage (7:1-40)
Instruction about Questionable Practices (8:1–11:1)

Instruction about Corporate Worship (11:2–14:40)
Instruction about the Resurrection (15:1-58)
Conclusion (16:1-24)

2 CORINTHIANS   The letter now called 2 Corinthians may
very well contain both the third and fourth letters that Paul sent
to Corinth. Paul makes reference to a third letter in 2 Corinthians
7:8: "I am no longer sorry that I sent that letter to you, though I
was sorry for a time, for I know that it was painful to you for a
little while." Apparently 1 Corinthians failed to remedy the problems at Corinth, and so did an ensuing visit to the church. The
Corinthian church was being troubled by some "false apostles,"
who were attempting to undermine Paul's authority. In order to
defend his apostolic position, Paul wrote the Corinthians a stern
letter, which may in fact be 2 Corinthians 10–13.

A little while later, when Paul was in Macedonia, Titus met
him with good news from the Corinthian church: The believers
had repented of their rebellion and were heeding Paul's instruction. Paul rejoiced at this news and sent yet another letter to the
church (A.D. 57). This final letter is now called 2 Corinthians
(possibly ending at chapter 9).

Second Corinthians is a very emotional, personal, and autobio-
graphical epistle. Paul freely expresses his emotions, showing
both depression and elation over the Corinthian church. Because
he regards the Corinthians as his dear children, Paul foregoes for-
mality and politeness, choosing instead to cut to the heart of the
issue. He rebukes them sharply for questioning his authority, yet
he just as easily praises them for repenting. Paul did not mince
words regarding his authority as an apostle—he fiercely defends
his commission by recounting his trials for the sake of the gospel. But Paul also reveals the anxiety he suffered while waiting
for the church's response to his defense.

Introduction (1:1-11)
The Nature of Paul's Apostolic Ministry (1:12–7:4)
Paul's Reconciliation with the Church (7:5-16)
Collection for the Christians at Jerusalem (8:1–9:15)
Paul's Defense of His Apostolic Authority (10:1–13:10)
Conclusion (13:11-13)

ROMANS Of all the epistles of Paul, the letter to the
Romans is the longest, the most elaborate, and the most systematic in design. It is more like a theological treatise than a personal letter, establishing a solid framework for understanding the
broad scope of the gospel.

Paul opens his discourse by discussing humanity's relationship to God. Paul describes the human race as violators of holy
law, which has been made evident in nature for pagans and in
Scripture for Jews. Once Paul establishes humanity's fallenness,
he offers a solution—the sacrifice of Jesus Christ. This sacrifice
for sin can only be obtained through faith. After a believer
receives remission for sin, new life is gained in Jesus Christ.
Paul uses several paragraphs to elaborate on each of these points.

Paul then moves into a discussion of Israel's place in God's
grand scheme of history. In many respects this section is perhaps
the most difficult to fully comprehend, as it sorts out God's purposes for allowing Israel (on the whole) to reject the gospel and
allowing the Gentiles to embrace it. Paul discusses the future
roles of Israel and the Gentile nations in the kingdom of God.

After this digression Paul returns to his earlier train of thought
and discusses the practical application of it. Paul finally concludes this lofty discourse with heartfelt salutations to several
believers in Rome.

It is almost certain that Paul wrote this epistle from Corinth in
the spring of A.D. 58. At that time he was on his way to Jerusa-

lem to deliver the collection from the Asian churches. After that he hoped to visit Rome on his way to Spain (15:23-28). Given his comments about longing to visit those in Rome (1:13), Paul probably had never yet been to the church in Rome until sometime after he had written to them. The church had apparently been established by other leaders or by those who had become believers during Peter's ministry at Pentecost.

While there was certainly a sizeable Jewish population in Rome at this time, it seems clear that Paul addressed his letter principally to Gentiles (1:13; 15:15-16). But it is equally evident that the church there included Jewish Christians as well, since Paul bases his entire argument upon principles from the Old Testament. Regardless of the letter's recipients, Paul's epistle to the Roman church provides the Christian church with a fairly systematic understanding of the gospel of Jesus Christ. Paul's framework in Romans has formed the backbone for much of Christian theology today.

Introduction (1:1-17)
All Humanity Needs Salvation (1:18–3:20)
Righteousness by Faith (3:21–5:21)
New Life in the Spirit (6:1–8:39)
Israel in the Plan of God (9:1–11:36)
Living as a Christian (12:1–15:13)
Conclusion (15:14–16:27)

EPHESIANS   The letter now addressed to the Ephesians was probably originally written as an encyclical—a letter circulated to several churches—for Asia, including Ephesus. This theory is supported by the fairly impersonal and universally applicable subject matter of the letter, despite Paul's three-year stay in Ephesus. There are no personal greetings or specific exhortations, unlike Paul's other letters. Paul addresses his readers as those who have only heard of his ministry (3:2), unlike the Ephesian believers. In addition, the earliest manuscripts of this epistle do not contain the words "in Ephesus" in the opening greeting. It is also possible that this letter is, in fact, the letter to the Laodiceans mentioned at the end of Colossians (4:15-16). Paul instructs the Colossians to trade letters with them, which lends support to the idea that it was written to be circulated among the churches.

Regardless of its intended recipients, the message of Ephesians remains clear: The universal church forms the unified body of Christ. The churches surrounding Ephesus were comprised of both Jewish and Gentile Christians (Acts 19:8-10). It was Paul's great desire to show them that they—as Jews and Greeks—were equal members in the body of Christ. In Christ all believers become one body with equal privileges for all (2:14-22). Paul explained that Jewish and Gentile Christians are comembers of the body and coheirs to God's promises in Christ (3:2-6). Since this epistle is Paul's treatise on the universal church, it is not encumbered with local issues. Instead, it soars above mundane affairs and presents a heavenly view of the church, as it fits into God's eternal plan.

Assuming that Ephesians was written at about the same time as Colossians, Paul probably penned this letter during the early part of his imprisonment in Rome (ca. A.D. 61). A few features of both letters suggest that Ephesians and Colossians were written around the same time. The two letters contain a significant number of parallel passages. Both letters also mention that Tychicus would be coming to visit the recipients.

Paul's presentation of the church reaches its pinnacle in this epistle. Paul depicts the church in ideal perfection, as seen from heaven—but not yet fully manifested on earth. Paul uses a wide variety of images to communicate God's grand conception of the church: It is Christ's body (1:22-23), God's masterpiece (2:10), the household of God (2:19), and the bride of Christ (5:23-32). Paul uses many other images as well. The letter to the Ephesians

provides the Christian church with a grand vision of itself
toward which it can continually grow.

Introduction (1:1-2)
God's Eternal Purpose for the Church (1:3-23)
The Creation of the Church (2:1-22)
The Mystery Explained (3:1-13)
Paul's Prayer for the Believers (3:14-21)
Unity of the Church (4:1-16)
Living as Children of Light (4:17–5:20)
Right Relationships in the Church (5:21–6:9)
Spiritual Warfare (6:10-20)
Conclusion (6:21-24)

COLOSSIANS   Paul's letter to the Colossians attempts to
counter various philosophical influences that had crept into the
church there. The text of Colossians suggests that the church had
been infiltrated by a syncretistic philosophical system that combined elements of legalistic Judaism, asceticism, and Gnosticism. The Gnostic element was the most pronounced, and Paul
gives it the greatest attention.

Colossae was a city in Asia Minor near Ephesus. The church
there was composed mainly of Gentiles (2:13). Apparently Paul
had never visited the Colossian church, but he had received word
about it through Epaphras, who may have founded the church.
Epaphras's report prompted Paul to write to the Colossians. This
letter was most likely written during Paul's first imprisonment at
Rome (A.D. 61). Paul probably also wrote Ephesians around this
time, as evidenced by a number of parallel passages with Colossians. The short epistle to Philemon, a member of the Colossian
church, was sent along with the letter to the Colossians.

In order to better understand Paul's reasoning in his letter to
the Colossians, it is essential to become familiar with Gnosti-

cism. While there were various forms of Gnosticism in Paul's day, a few basic concepts were generally assumed by all of them. All Gnostics believed matter to be inherently evil, which led to a belief in mediating beings between God and creation. If God was truly good, then he could not possibly have anything to do with evil creation. Therefore there must be a series of "aeons," or emanations from God, each a little more distant from him and each having a little less deity. At the end of this chain of intermediate beings there is an emanation possessing enough deity to create a world but removed far enough from God that his creative activities could not compromise the perfect purity of God. In light of these beliefs, the Christian concept of the Incarnation in Jesus Christ caused a problem for Gnostics. Either Jesus was not fully divine, or else he must have only appeared to be human.

In order to combat this distortion of Jesus Christ's true identity, Paul emphasizes the all-sufficiency and preeminence of Christ. Throughout this short epistle, Paul uses almost thirty different images to describe Christ, including the redeemer (1:14), God's visible image (1:15), the firstborn of all creation (1:15), the head of the body (1:18), the beginning (1:18), the firstborn from the dead (1:18), the preeminent one (1:18), the embodiment of all God's fullness (1:19), the mediator of reconciliation (1:20), the hope of glory (1:27), the mystery of God (2:2), the head of every ruler and authority (2:10), the reality of all shadows (2:16-17), the one hidden in God (3:3), our life (3:4), the one who will appear with us in glory (3:4), and the forgiver (3:13). Paul leaves no questions as to the preeminence of Christ.

The style of this epistle is unique; many Greek phrases occur here that are found nowhere else in the New Testament. Paul's lofty and elaborate discourse corresponds to the majestic nature of his theme—the majesty of Christ's person and office. Paul intentionally uses many phrases belonging to Gnostic philosophy in order to portray Jesus Christ as the answer to the Colossians' questions.

Introduction (1:1-14)
The Supremacy of Christ (1:15-23)
Paul's Labor for the Church (1:24–2:5)
Dealing with Heresies (2:6-23)
The New Life versus the Old (3:1–4:6)
Conclusion (4:7-18)

PHILEMON   Paul's brief letter to Philemon, a member of the Colossian church, provides a glimpse into the personal interactions of Paul and other believers. This epistle, probably written on a single leaf of papyrus, makes a personal plea to Philemon to welcome back his runaway slave, Onesimus. Paul even appears to do a bit of subtle arm-twisting to encourage Philemon to forgive Onesimus.

Paul's letter to Philemon is closely linked with his letter to the Colossians. The two epistles include salutations from the same people (except for Justus). Paul mentions in both letters that he is a prisoner. It is also almost certain, therefore, that the letter to Philemon was sent along with the Colossian letter, as Onesimus returned to his owner. This would mean that the letter to Philemon was written from Rome during Paul's imprisonment around A.D. 61.

Apparently Onesimus had run away from Philemon sometime earlier and had become a Christian under Paul's ministry. Onesimus seems to have become an assistant to Paul, until it was decided that he should return to his owner. Paul appeals to Philemon "because of [their] love," although he makes it very clear that he could rightfully order Philemon to receive Onesimus back. He points out that Onesimus is now Philemon's brother in Christ. Paul offers to repay Philemon for anything that Onesimus owes him, while mentioning that Philemon owes Paul his very life. Paul ends the epistle by asking Philemon to prepare a place for him to stay, because Paul expected to be set free from prison soon and planned to visit Colossae.

Greetings (1-3)
Thanksgiving and Prayer (4-7)
Paul's Plea for Onesimus (8-21)
Conclusion (22-25)

PHILIPPIANS   Paul's letter to the Philippian believers is perhaps the warmest and most encouraging of all his letters. The object of the epistle is general: Paul wants to thank the Philippians for their contribution to him and to express his love and sympathy for them.

Although some scholars have argued that it was written in Caesarea or Ephesus, Philippians was probably written in Rome near the end of Paul's first imprisonment there (A.D. 62). The reference to "Caesar's palace" (4:22) and to the "palace guard" (1:13) tend to support this location.

Philippi was a leading Macedonian city and a Roman colony. Its inhabitants were transplanted from Rome and were given the full rights of Roman citizenship. They were not subject to the regional government, and they maintained their own senate and magistrates. Paul founded the church there, along with Silas and Timothy (Acts 16:12), and visited it a couple of times throughout his ministry. The church probably consisted mostly of Gentiles, since there were not even enough Jews to form a synagogue when Paul first arrived. Paul's sufferings at Philippi (Acts 16:19) strengthened ties between him and his Philippian converts, who were also exposed to trials for the gospel's sake. They alone sent supplies for Paul's needs on several occasions (Philippians 4:10-18).

As Paul wrote to thank the Philippians for their gift, he opened his letter with details about his condition as a prisoner and about Epaphroditus's condition. Epaphroditus probably held a leading office in the Philippian church, perhaps as an elder. He had become ill for a time and had almost died, but then he recovered. Paul also exhorted the Philippians to imitate Jesus Christ. He used what was probably an early Christian hymn to describe the humility and glorification of Christ (2:6-11).

The second section of the letter cautions the believers against those who want to impose Mosaic law upon them. Paul reveals that he has every reason to boast in his Jewish heritage, but he refuses to do so because it is of little account when compared to the value of knowing Jesus Christ.

In the third section, Paul gently admonishes a few individuals and the church in general, and he thanks them for their gift. Overall, it should be said that this epistle reveals Paul's strong desire to know Christ, to be like him, and to glorify him—whether by life or by death. The letter to the Philippians contains no bold censures but focuses instead upon encouraging the church to become like Christ.

Introduction (1:1-11)
Paul's Personal Circumstances (1:12-26)
Living the Christian Life (1:27–2:18)
Paul's Coworkers, Timothy and Epaphroditus (2:19-30)
Pursuing the Knowledge of Christ (3:1–4:1)
Exhortations to Unity, Joy, and Peace (4:2-9)
Thanks for the Philippians' Gift (4:10-20)
Conclusion (4:21-23)

The Pastoral Epistles
The epistles known as 1 Timothy, 2 Timothy, and Titus are called the Pastoral Epistles because they are letters of instruction to par-

ticular church leaders—namely, Timothy and Titus. Paul's authorship of the Pastoral Epistles is a topic of much debate. Several reasons have been posited against Pauline authorship, but none of them are conclusive. Some have cited that the book of Acts does not include events surrounding the writing of these letters. While this is true, it does not disprove Pauline authorship. Rather, it shows that Paul could have written the Pastoral Epistles after his first imprisonment (which is where the narrative of Acts ends).

Other scholars have noted that the style of the Pastoral Epistles is different from the style of the other Pauline letters. It is evident in Paul's other letters, however, that his style passed through various phases of development. His early epistles are all similar in style and vocabulary, while his later epistles differ from them. Likewise, the Pastoral Epistles resemble each other while differing from the earlier letters. The occasions and conditions for each writing brought forth new expressions to meet the need. In addition, Paul may have used an amanuensis (personal scribe) to help compile the Pastoral Epistles.

The seemingly developed system of church structure has also been given as a case against Pauline authorship. The mere mention of "overseers," however, does not necessarily relegate these letters to the second century. Throughout the Pastoral Epistles, *overseer* seems to be synonymous with *elder*. Likewise in Philippians 1:1, Paul greets the "elders," ("overseers") along with the deacons.

The Pastoral Epistles provide the Christian church with mature insight from the aged apostle to the Gentiles. Paul instructs Timothy and Titus in much the same way as a father teaches his maturing children.

1 TIMOTHY   Paul's first letter to Timothy was written to encourage the young leader to take care of the Ephesian church while Paul was absent. Many scholars believe that 1 Timothy was written sometime between Paul's first and second imprisonment in Rome (ca. A.D. 63). Paul may have been in Corinth at the time he wrote this letter.

In this letter Paul directs Timothy to combat teaching that strays from the apostle's instruction (1:3-20). He gives Timothy instructions for worship in church meetings, for the selection of qualified elders and deacons, and for the appointment of widows to church service. Paul also advises the young church leader regarding how he should relate to older members of the church, as well as to female members. This is followed by a personal appeal to Timothy, as a man of God, to fight the good fight of faith until the time of the Lord's appearing (6:11-16).

> Salutation (1:1-2)
> Warning against False Teachers (1:3-11)
> God's Grace to Paul (1:12-20)
> Instructions on Worship (2:1-15)
> Qualifications for Leaders (3:1-16)
> Instructions to Timothy (4:1-16)
> Advice about Widows, Elders, and Slaves (5:1–6:3)
> False Teachers and Lovers of Money (6:3-10)
> Paul's Final Exhortation (6:11-21)

TITUS The purpose of Paul's letter to Titus was to instruct Titus in leading the churches on the island of Crete. Titus, a Greek Gentile, was a young coworker with Paul. Paul probably wrote to Titus from Corinth sometime after his first imprisonment (ca. A.D. 65).

During Titus's ministry on Crete, several corrupt elements began to emerge in the churches there. These false teachings were similar to those noticed under Timothy's ministry in Ephesus: Jewish legalism, elements of Gnosticism, and immoral behavior. Paul tried to guide Titus in overcoming these influences. He reiterated the qualifications of elders and explained the virtues that should be displayed among believers. He also directed Titus to encourage the Cretans to adorn the gospel by living industrious, honest lives. The stereotype of Cretans at the time was not very admirable, as evidenced by Paul's quote from the Cretan poet Epimenides. Paul wanted the Cretan church to overcome this dubious reputation and honor God.

Salutation (1:1-4)
Qualifications for Leaders (1:5-9)
Warning against False Teachers (1:10-16)
Right Living in the Church (2:1-15)
Right Living in Society (3:1-11)
Conclusion (3:12-15)

2 TIMOTHY   The final letter of Paul in the New Testament is his second letter to Timothy. Nearing the end of his life, Paul charges Timothy with some final duties as a young leader of the church. As he instructs Timothy to hold fast to the sound teaching of the apostles, Paul, in a sense, is passing on the baton of the Christian faith.

After Paul's release from his first imprisonment in Rome (ca. A.D. 63), Paul wrote to Timothy and Titus from Corinth. At some point Paul visited Troas, where he left some books and a cloak with Carpus (4:13). Eventually Paul returned to Rome, where he was imprisoned a second time, possibly on charges of setting fire to Rome (A.D. 64) or of propagating a novel and unlawful religion in the empire. This imprisonment was much harsher than the first, as 2 Timothy indicates (2:9). From his prison Paul wrote this second letter to Timothy shortly before his execution (ca. A.D. 68). It is not certain where Timothy was at this time. Based on the greetings and references in the letter, it is possible that Timothy was still in Ephesus.

As the time of Paul's execution drew near, he grew anxious to see his disciple, Timothy. Paul asks Timothy to come visit him soon and to bring Mark (another of Paul's coworkers) with him (4:9-13). He also asks Timothy to bring the cloak and books that he left in Troas. Paul seems uncertain, however, that Timothy will arrive in time, and so he shares some final words in his letter. He warns Timothy against heresies that were infecting the churches and encourages him to preach the Scriptures, promoting godly living and spiritual perseverance. He exhorts Timothy to pass on the teachings of the apostles to faithful believers.

As he penned his final words to Timothy, Paul encouraged his young disciple to press on in the faith, as he himself had done. Near the end of his letter, Paul included what could be considered an inspiring epitaph for any believer: "As for me, my life has already been poured out as an offering to God. The time of my death is near. I have fought a good fight, I have finished the race, and I have remained faithful" (4:6-7).

Salutation (1:1-2)
Exhortation to Faithfulness (1:3-18)
A Call to Fervency and Endurance (2:1-13)
A Workman Approved by God (2:14-26)
Facing Difficult Times (3:1-17)
Paul's Final Words (4:1-8)
Conclusion (4:9-22)

The General Epistles

The New Testament concludes with several books that are called the General Epistles. They are also known as the Catholic (universal) or the Common Epistles. This might be somewhat misleading, however, because some of the General Epistles are addressed to specific readers (1 Peter, 2 John, 3 John). The common characteristic of all of these letters is that they are non-Pauline epistles.

JAMES   The epistle of James to the "twelve tribes in the dispersion" was written like a collection of wise Jewish teachings, much like Jesus' Sermon on the Mount. There are striking similarities in language and style between this epistle and Jesus' sermon. James even uses the word *synagogue* rather than *church* as the place of meeting for believers (2:2), betraying his Jewish background. Nevertheless, the letter does ground itself as a Christian epistle (1:1; 2:1).

The Jewish tone of this letter lends strong support to the traditional claim that James, the brother of Jesus and elder of the Jerusalem church, was its author. He would certainly be very familiar with Jewish styles of writing, and the Jerusalem church was described in Acts 21:18-24 as taking the law of Moses very seriously. Though James was not one of the original twelve apostles, his close relation to Jesus gave him similar authority, and this is what enabled the epistle to be included in the New Testament canon. The letter's very Jewish tone and its salutation to "the twelve tribes," combined with its complete silence about the Jewish/Gentile controversy, lead many scholars to date this letter very early. It may even have been written as early as A.D. 45.

This letter discusses the gospel in relation to the Law, which the Jews so revered. As Paul's epistles reflect on doctrines emanating from Christ's death and resurrection, so James's epistle focuses on Jesus' teachings. In both the Sermon on the Mount and the epistle of James, true fulfillment of the law flows out of genuine love on the part of the believer. For James, practice, not profession, is the test of true obedience (2:17; 4:17). Likewise, faith without works is seen as dead and useless. James uses the Old Testament figure Abraham as an example of one who was justified not by faith alone but by works, when he offered Isaac as a sacrifice to God (2:20-23). It is interesting to note that Paul used the very same character to prove what appears to be just the opposite point: Abraham was justified because he believed God's promises, not because he had done anything (Romans 3–4).

This apparent tension between James and Paul has caused many Christians difficulty over the centuries. Martin Luther is perhaps the most noted example. He once described James's letter as "an epistle of straw . . . destitute of an evangelical character." Since Luther's time, however, many scholars have argued that James does not oppose the doctrine of justification by faith, as taught by Paul. While looking at justification from distinct standpoints, Paul and James mutually complement each other's definitions. Paul saw faith as producing justification, which in turn produces good works. James saw good works as the genuine proof that one had faith and was therefore justified.

> Salutation (1:1)
> Trials and Temptations (1:2-18)
> Doers of the Word (1:19-27)
> Rebuking Favoritism (2:1-13)
> Faith and Works (2:14-26)
> Controlling the Tongue (3:1-12)
> Two Kinds of Wisdom (3:13-18)
> Warnings against Worldliness and Wealth (4:1–5:6)
> Concluding Exhortations (5:7-20)

HEBREWS This nameless epistle, later entitled "to the Hebrews," reflects upon the superiority of Christ and the new covenant over Judaism and the old covenant. For some believers, the excitement of Christianity began to wane as time and persecution dragged on, and many considered reverting to Judaism. In order to dissuade them, the author of Hebrews used the Old Testament to show that Jesus Christ has fulfilled and superseded the old covenant of Judaism.

The identity of the author of Hebrews has been anyone's guess over the centuries. The letter does not open with the standard introduction that identifies the author. It is clear, however, that the author was highly fluent in Greek, as evidenced by the myriad of refined phrases and literary devices used throughout the letter. Much of the author's reasoning suggests a penchant for Alexandrian modes of thought. While the actual syntax and phrases of the letter do not resemble Paul's, the general concepts conveyed do resemble the apostle's. This fact, as well as the author's familiarity with Timothy (13:23), suggest that the author was at least a close associate of Paul. These criteria would narrow the field of likely candidates to Apollos, Barnabas, Luke, or possibly even Priscilla. This lack of agreement over the epistle's authorship, however, only serves to emphasize the strength of its content. It is beautifully written, brilliantly structured, and genuinely communicated.

The date of the epistle's composition and the believers to whom it was written are also open to question. Many scholars suspect that it was written to believers in Rome, given the greetings from Christians "from Italy" (13:24). Other scholars posit Alexandria as the destination, since the Muratorian Canon mentions an "epistle to the Alexandrians" in its list. The author's assumption of ongoing priestly practices suggests that the letter was written before the destruction of the temple in A.D. 70.

The epistle to the Hebrews opens by showing that the New Covenant is superior to the old by virtue of Jesus Christ's superiority over the angels and the prophets. Jesus is superior to Moses as well, and yet he was able to identify with humanity, since he became fully human. Jesus is the perfect High Priest, as shown by the Old Testament passages about Melchizedek, the priest to whom Abraham gave a tithe. All this contributes to

Jesus' perfect sacrifice for sin, which replaces the sacrifices of the old covenant. If all this is true, then the readers must not fall away from following Christ, but instead they must continue in faith, as did the great heroes of the past. The readers are then given some final warnings and instructions in how to live as Christians in a hostile world.

The letter to the Hebrews provides the church with a brilliant portrayal of the preeminence of Jesus Christ. Yet the book captures the humanity of Jesus just as vividly. Few other New Testament books so artfully and effectively utilize Old Testament concepts to illuminate the significance of Jesus Christ.

Prologue (1:1-4)
Jesus Christ, the Superior Messenger (1:5–2:18)
Jesus Christ, the Superior Apostle (3:1–4:13)
Jesus Christ, the Superior Priest (4:14–7:28)
Jesus Christ's Better Covenant (8:1–9:28)
Jesus Christ's Better Sacrifice (10:1-39)
Faith, the Better Way (11:1–12:29)
Conclusion (13:1-25)

1 PETER This letter was written to Christians who were living as "foreigners" in Asia Minor. These Christians were being persecuted and ostracized by their pagan neighbors. The epistle consoles the persecuted believers and prepares them for even harder times. These sufferings would perfect the believers' faith and purify their souls. The letter also encourages all believers— husbands and wives, masters and slaves, elders and laity—to live godly lives in the presence of unbelievers, thereby giving testimony to Jesus Christ.

Peter identifies himself at the opening of the letter as the author, although he notes that Silvanus actually wrote it down for him. Silvanus's influence accounts for the very refined Greek used in this letter. It is clear that the author, who is a "witness to the sufferings of Christ" (5:1), is the apostle Peter himself. Peter was probably in Rome at the time he wrote this epistle, since "Babylon" (5:13) was the usual Christian code word for "Rome" in the first century. This word is also used in Revelation 14:8 and 16:19 as a code word for Rome. This would fit the strong tradition that Peter ministered primarily in Rome. The fairly developed churches and the persecutions mentioned in the letter suggest a later date for the letter's composition, possibly around A.D. 63.

The regions to which Peter addressed this letter are listed in the order that a messenger would follow to deliver mail in Asia Minor. Most of the churches in these provinces (Pontus, Galatia, Cappadocia, Asia, and Bithynia) were started by Paul and his associates. These churches probably consisted primarily of Jewish Christians, but they also had Gentile Christians as well.

Salutation (1:1-2)
A Holy People for God (1:3–2:12)
Learning to Be Submissive (2:13–3:7)
Suffering as Christians (3:8–5:11)
Conclusion (5:12-14)

2 PETER The epistle called 2 Peter is markedly different from the first letter attributed to this apostle. This second epistle warns readers against false teachers and encourages them to grow in the knowledge of Jesus Christ.

Peter's authorship of this epistle has been questioned throughout the centuries for several reasons. These reasons include: (1) The epistle was not readily accepted in the early church; (2) the writing style of this epistle is different from 1 Peter; (3) Peter's name has been connected with many Gnostic pseudepigrapha *(The Gospel of Peter, The Acts of Peter,*

The Teaching of Peter, The Letter of Peter to James, The Preaching of Peter); and (4) 2 Peter shares some of the same material found in Jude.

Since Silvanus is not mentioned in 2 Peter, he probably did not help write this letter as he did with 1 Peter. This could account for the differences in writing style between the two letters. Perhaps Peter wrote this letter himself. If he did, it was probably between A.D. 66 and 68, just prior to his martyrdom. Peter may have been in Rome at the time he wrote this generically addressed epistle.

One interesting note about this letter is its use of apocalyptic and extrabiblical imagery. It vividly describes demons that are chained in darkness awaiting judgment. The letter closes with a warning to lead lives that anticipate the return of the Lord.

Salutation (1:1-2)
Instructions for Living Godly Lives (1:3-11)
The Authenticity of Peter's Message (1:12-21)
Warning against False Teachers (2:1-22)
The Coming of the Lord (3:1-16)
Conclusion (3:17-18)

JUDE   This short letter was written to counter false teaching that was infecting the early church. The epistle condemns those who reject the authority of the apostles and live self-indulgent, lustful lives.

The author identifies himself as Jude, a brother of James. It is assumed that James is the brother of Jesus, and, therefore, Jude must also be a brother of Jesus. The fact that this letter shares a large amount of material with 2 Peter does not help in dating its composition, since it is not clear which author borrowed from which letter. The letter appears to have been an open letter to the church in general, rather than to any specific church.

This epistle also contains some extrabiblical imagery, and it even quotes from the apocryphal book of *1 Enoch*. Though this letter is one of the shortest in the New Testament, it contains perhaps the most elaborate of all benedictions.

Introduction (1-2)
Warning against False Teachers (3-16)
Standing Firm in the Faith (17-23)
Conclusion (24-25)

1 JOHN   Three letters are traditionally attributed to the apostle John, based upon their linguistic and theological similarities with the Gospel of John. All three letters were probably written at about the same time, possibly before John penned his Gospel (ca. A.D. 85). John may have been in Ephesus as he wrote, since he served as an elder there for many years.

The first letter is very different from the typical epistle format of the first century. It skips the introduction, leaving the letter unsigned and unaddressed. Instead, it starts right into its very concise yet very significant message concerning the person of Jesus Christ.

This first epistle was prompted by a heretical faction that had developed within the church. Apparently this faction had eventually left the church, but seeds of doubt still remained in the minds of many believers (2:18-19). The faction had distorted the apostles' teachings about the person of Christ, denying that Jesus Christ had actually come in the flesh (4:1-3). It is very possible that this heresy was a form of Docetism, which asserted that Christ only "appeared" to come in the flesh.

In order to redirect the believers in the right way, John urges his readers to walk in the light with God and with fellow Christians, to confess their sins, to love God and others, to purify themselves from worldly lusts, to follow the Spirit of truth in discerning false teachings, and to esteem Jesus Christ as the true God. John stresses the importance of fellowship in order to safeguard against further factions and heresies in the future.

Prologue (1:1-4)
Fellowship with the Father and the Son (1:5–2:29)
Love among God's People (3:1–4:21)
True Faith (5:1-12)
Conclusion (5:13-21)

2 JOHN   This brief second letter of the apostle John contains much of the same language and thoughts of the first letter. In typical letter format, 2 John opens by identifying "the Elder" (John) as its author and addressing itself to "the chosen lady and to her children." The corporate tone of the letter suggests that "the chosen lady" refers to a church rather than an actual woman.

Salutation (1-3)
Encouragement and Warnings (4-11)
Conclusion (12-13)

3 JOHN   The third letter of John ("the Elder") was written to Gaius. Although the New Testament mentions several men with the name Gaius, it would be difficult to say which, if any, of these was the recipient of this epistle. In any event, John penned this short letter to give notice of his upcoming visit to the church in Gaius's locality. A certain man named Diotrephes had taken control of the church and was refusing to receive John or anyone sent by him. Diotrephes even expelled people from the church who accepted anyone sent there by John. John warns the believers that he will deal with Diotrephes when he arrives. John commends Demetrius for his upright Christian life.

. . . . .THE GOSPELS AND ACTS

The life and ministry of Jesus Christ forms the core of the Christian faith, so it is important for believers to learn about him. During the first several decades following Jesus' death and resurrection, the oral traditions of the apostles were the most reliable sources for learning about Jesus. The New Testament books repeatedly note the importance of the apostles' ministry as they worked to accurately inform the church about Jesus Christ. All teachings about Jesus had to conform to the apostles' oral accounts.

As time wore on, however, the apostles grew older and some passed away, leaving fewer and fewer sources for reliable information about Jesus. The solution was to write down the apostles' teachings in order to preserve their authoritative message for later generations. These written accounts came to be known as "Gospels."

Opinions differ about whether or not the gospel was a new literary form in the first century. Some scholars argue that the gospel as a literary form has no real parallel outside of the New Testament writings and should not be compared with concurrent Jewish or Greek literature. Others insist that the gospel resembles other biographies or hero stories of Greek and Jewish literature.

While it is true that the Gospels are unique in many respects, especially regarding their assertion that Jesus is the Messiah, they do seem to contain some features of other ancient biographies. It would be only natural for a first-century writer to present a collection of oral traditions about Jesus in a form that readers would recognize and understand. Gentile readers, familiar with biographies of great men, likely would have understood the Gospels as such. Likewise, Jewish readers probably would have associated the Gospels with the familiar hero narratives of the Old Testament, for the Gospels are, indeed, hero stories on a grand scale. They are an excellent example of narrative built on the life of an exemplary protagonist whose acts and words are treasured and celebrated.

It is important to recognize, however, that the Gospel writers truly did believe in the content of their narratives. They were not merely spinning yarns about a fictitious legend. They believed that Jesus really is the Messiah, and their stories were written to communicate this all-important message.

MARK The Gospel according to Mark is probably the earliest of the existing Gospels. Matthew and Luke probably used Mark as a source for their Gospels, which would account for the large amount of verbatim parallels among them. These three accounts are commonly called the synoptic Gospels.

The title of this Gospel, "according to Mark," almost certainly refers to John Mark of Acts 12:25. He was the nephew of Barnabas, an early Jewish Christian in the church at Jerusalem. The Roman name "Mark" was perhaps a badge of Roman citizenship, as in Paul's case, or it may have been adopted when he left Jerusalem to serve the Gentile church in Antioch. Mark has a history of affiliation with the apostle Peter. When an angel of the Lord freed Peter from prison, the apostle went directly to "the home of Mary, the mother of John Mark" (Acts 12:12). Peter also mentions in his first letter that his "son" Mark was with him in "Babylon" (5:13), a code name for Rome. Tradition holds that Mark ministered in Rome with Peter in his later years and compiled his Gospel from Peter's teachings about Jesus Christ (ca. A.D. 63). This tradition is further supported by the Gospel's tendency to focus on Peter's words and deeds (8:29-33; 9:4-7; 10:28-31; 14:29-31, 66-72), and even on Peter himself (16:7).

Several features about this Gospel suggest that it was written for Gentile believers in Rome. Mark is careful to explain Jewish customs (7:3-4; 14:12; 15:42), to translate Aramaic expressions into Greek (3:17; 5:41; 7:11, 34; 15:22, 34), to use Latin terms and measurements (5:9; 6:27, 48; 12:15, 42; 13:35; 15:16, 39), and to record a profession of faith from a Roman centurion at the cross (15:39).

Since Mark's audience was composed primarily of believers, who should have already been familiar with the major events of Jesus' life, he did not attempt to write an exhaustive biography. Rather, Mark used an abbreviated account of the life and works of Jesus to present him as the Messiah and to provide the church with a dynamic model of Christian life and service—especially in the face of intense opposition.

The Gospel of Mark opens with the preaching of John the Baptist and the baptism of Jesus. Almost immediately after this event, Jesus begins performing miracles and preaching about the kingdom of God. Jesus is constantly on the move throughout the narrative, and his teaching is interspersed throughout his miracles. Mark notes that Jesus taught mostly in parables. Mark seems to regard Jesus' actions, however, as of greatest significance.

Throughout the book, the Son of God, the Messiah, is constantly presented as very much human. Likewise, Jesus constantly points to God rather than to himself, further emphasizing his humanity. Halfway through the book Jesus finally reveals his identity as the Messiah, but he warns his disciples that he must go to Jerusalem to be crucified. He is hailed as king upon entering Jerusalem, but then he is killed one week later.

The Gospel closes with the story of Jesus' resurrection, but it appears to have been left incomplete (according to the most reliable manuscripts). The story ends as the women leave the empty

tomb in fear and tell no one. It is possible that the last pages of
the Gospel were lost very soon after they were written.

At the time this Gospel was written (ca. A.D. 63), the Christians in Rome were living under the reign of Nero, who despised
Christianity. Many Christians were being persecuted and even
killed for their faith. The Gospel of Mark would have greatly
encouraged the Roman believers, since it describes how Jesus
labored in the face of constant opposition and resolutely determined to fulfill his destiny on the cross. Mark's Gospel also
develops a theology about Jesus as God's Son and as humanity's
servant, but the primary purpose of the Gospel was to preserve a
record of the life and actions of Jesus the Messiah.

> Opening Events of Jesus' Ministry (1:1-13)
> Jesus' Early Galilean Ministry (1:14–3:6)
> Second Phase of Galilean Ministry (3:7–7:23)
> Third Phase of Galilean Ministry (7:24–9:50)
> Jesus' Journey to Jerusalem (10:1-52)
> Jesus' Final Week in Jerusalem (11:1–15:47)
> Jesus' Resurrection (16:1-8)
> The Longer Ending of Mark (16:9-20)

MATTHEW   Though it is clear that the Gospel of Matthew
includes a significant amount of material from the Gospel of
Mark, it is difficult to determine just when the Gospel was compiled. There is even debate over which Gospel came first. The
early church recognized Matthew as the first Gospel and placed
it first in the New Testament canon. The genealogy that introduces this Gospel also provided a convenient segue from the Old
Testament to the New Testament. Many scholars today, however,
place the date of Matthew's composition after Mark, possibly
around A.D. 65.

The early church fathers recognized the apostle Matthew as

the author of this Gospel. The title "according to Matthew" could have been added later, so it is difficult to be certain if Matthew was indeed the author. Since there is little evidence that significantly calls this into question, however, there is little reason to question the tradition that the educated tax collector is the author of this Gospel.

Assuming that Matthew was written after Mark, it appears that the author used Mark as a framework for the life and actions of Jesus and expanded upon it with additional information and sayings of Jesus. Many scholars argue that Matthew, as well as Luke, made use of a collection of Aramaic sayings of Jesus as he compiled his Gospel in Greek. While this is possible, it is still debated. Nevertheless, it is clear that Matthew placed a great deal of emphasis on Jesus' parables and teachings, as well as his deeds.

Matthew's Gospel has been described as the Gospel written for the Jews. Its Jewish focus and flavor are evident throughout the book. Matthew contains more than fifty Old Testament quotations and more than seventy-five other allusions. Matthew opens his Gospel by tracing Jesus' descent from Abraham and David. Matthew uses Jewish terminology and does not bother to explain Jewish customs. To do so was unnecessary because his readers were predominantly Jewish. Another Jewish theme in this Gospel is Jesus' image as the Messiah who fulfills the Old Testament prophecies.

While it is fairly certain, then, that Matthew wrote this Gospel to convince Jews that Jesus is the Messiah and that he has ushered in the kingdom of heaven, it is also clear that Matthew wanted to emphasize the Gentiles' inclusion in the kingdom. Jesus is presented as God's servant sent to the Gentiles (12:18-21), and the apostles are sent by Jesus to make disciples of all the nations (28:19). The kingdom of heaven would be filled with Jews and Gentiles alike through the work of Jesus Christ.

According to Matthew's presentation, the kingdom of heaven

arrived on earth with the birth of Jesus Christ, and it would continue to be revealed in various phases. The advent of Jesus marked the first manifestation of the kingdom. To believe in Jesus as the Messiah granted the believer entrance into the kingdom. The final arrival of the kingdom was postponed by the Jews' rejection of Jesus (21:42-43). Much of Jesus' language concerning the kingdom indicates a future reign. In the meantime, the kingdom will be coexistent with the church (16:18-19) and will reside in people's hearts (13:3-23). Eventually the kingdom of heaven will be displayed in full power and glory on the earth after Jesus Christ has returned.

Jesus' Birth and Infancy (1:1–2:23)
The Beginning of Jesus' Ministry (3:1–4:25)
The Sermon on the Mount (5:1–7:29)
Jesus' Miracles (8:1–9:34)
Jesus Sends Out the Twelve Disciples (9:35–10:42)
The Claims of Jesus (11:1–12:50)
Parables of the Kingdom of Heaven (13:1-52)
Jesus Rejected and John the Baptist Beheaded
   (13:53–14:12)
Jesus Leaves Herod's Dominion (14:13–17:27)
Jesus' Teachings on Forgiveness (18:1-35)
Jesus' Journey to Jerusalem (19:1–20:34)
Jesus' Final Week in Jerusalem (21:1–28:10)
Events Following the Resurrection (28:11-20)

LUKE The Gospel of Luke and the book of Acts were written as a two-part sequel sometime between A.D. 60 and 70. Acts was written shortly after Paul's two-year imprisonment (ca. A.D. 60–62) mentioned in Acts 28:30.

The preface to the Gospel indicates that Luke was not an eyewitness or immediate disciple of Jesus; he received his information from others who had been with Jesus. Luke carried out extensive research and then wrote an orderly account about Jesus.

This Gospel, as well as the book of Acts, traditionally has been ascribed to Luke the physician. Although he is not mentioned by name in either of these books, Luke is the most reasonable candidate for authorship. He was an associate of Paul throughout his ministry to the Gentiles. Luke himself was a Gentile and would have been fluent in Greek. This would account for the highly refined grammar and vocabulary of Luke and Acts. The similarities in content between the Gospel of Luke and Paul's writings lend further support to Luke's authorship. Luke's account of the Last Supper is exactly the same as Paul's (cf. Luke 22:19-20 with 1 Corinthians 11:23-25). When Paul mentions the post-Resurrection appearances, he recalls that Jesus was first seen by Peter and then by the Twelve (1 Corinthians 15:4-5). Luke alone among the Gospel writers affirms that Jesus appeared first to Peter and then to the Twelve (Luke 24:34).

Since Paul was the apostle to the Gentiles, it is no surprise that his associate, Luke, would write a Gospel for the Gentiles—specifically for a Gentile convert named Theophilus. Luke penned an account to verify the facts of Jesus' life and ministry and, in so doing, to establish and fortify Theophilus's faith. Of course Luke's readership would extend beyond Theophilus to many readers with many needs, but this Gospel was initially aimed to help Gentile converts become grounded in their newfound faith. Like Matthew, Luke appears to have used Mark as a framework for his Gospel, and he, too, includes material that may have come from a collection of Aramaic teachings of Jesus.

When the Gospel of Luke is compared to the other Gospels, certain emphases become apparent. These features become even more apparent when Luke's sequel, the book of Acts, is taken into account. Luke was keenly interested in the inclusion of the whole world in the gospel of Jesus Christ. Many of Jesus' parables reflect this concern for Gentiles as well as Jews. Luke also focuses upon individual believers, social outcasts, women, children, and the poor. Luke highlights prayer and the work of the Holy Spirit, and this results in a striking note of joyfulness and praise throughout his Gospel.

Jesus' Background and Early Life (1:1–2:52)
The Ministry of John the Baptist (3:1-20)
The Beginning of Jesus' Ministry (3:21–4:13)
Jesus' Ministry in Galilee (4:14–9:50)
Jesus' Journey to Jerusalem (9:51–19:44)
Jesus' Final Week in Jerusalem (19:45–23:56)
Jesus' Resurrection and Appearances (24:1-53)

ACTS The book of Acts, in addition to the third Gospel, was written by Luke shortly after Paul's first imprisonment in Rome (ca. A.D. 60–62). Originally Luke and Acts were written as a two-volume work for a believer named Theophilus (Acts 1:1-3). During the second century, the Gospel of Luke was separated from Acts when it was added to the three other Gospels to form a single collection. It is important to remember, however, that the two books were written as a single work and therefore complement each other.

As in the Gospel of Luke, the language of Acts resembles refined classical Greek mingled with Semitic phrases from time to time. Luke includes himself at several places throughout the narrative, as is noted by his use of *we* in reference to Paul's entourage (16:10-17; 20:5-15; 21:1-18; 27:1–28:16).

The book of Acts is basically a synopsis of early church history. The book divides itself into six sections by inserting a verse after each section that makes a positive statement concerning the spread of the gospel and the church.

The book of Acts (sometimes called "the Acts of the Apostles") begins with the outpouring of the promised Holy Spirit at Pentecost. The apostles (formerly called disciples) immediately begin proclaiming the gospel of Jesus Christ and performing miracles through the Holy Spirit. The apostles begin their activities in Jerusalem, expand to Asia Minor and Europe, and eventually reach Rome, covering most of the Roman Empire over time. The first half of the book focuses on the work of Peter and the other apostles. The second half follows Paul on his missionary journeys, giving a general overview of the growth of the early church. The gospel is first presented only to Jews, and some receive it. Others reject it, and this precipitates Paul's move to minister primarily among the Gentiles. The church dramatically expands among the Gentiles. A critical point in the narrative is the Jerusalem Council, which was formed in order to resolve the debate over the role of Mosaic law among Gentile Christians. After the council decides not to impose the entire Mosaic law upon Gentile believers, the church expands even more. Along the way, Paul is continually plagued by persecution, by danger, and by Jews who are zealous to uphold Mosaic law.

The Church in Jerusalem (1:1–6:7)
The Church throughout Palestine (6:8–9:31)
The Church in Antioch (9:32–12:24)
The Church throughout Asia Minor (12:25–16:5)
The Church throughout Europe (16:6–19:20)
The Church at Rome (19:21–28:31)

JOHN   The Gospel of John was the last of the four Gospels to be written. It is markedly different from the three synoptic Gospels in several ways. The basic plot structure does not follow the book of Mark. For example, Jesus travels to Jerusalem several times throughout the Gospel of John, unlike the synoptic accounts, where a single trip to Jerusalem provides the climax of the story. John's account also focuses predominantly on Jesus' teaching and the theological significance of his life and actions.

Several theological and stylistic similarities have convinced many scholars that the author of this Gospel is the same one who wrote the epistles of John. While the writer is not specifically named in the Gospel, he gives every indication that he is indeed John, "the disciple whom Jesus loved." This apostle was one of the three disciples (along with Peter and James, John's brother) who were especially close to Jesus. John is thought to have ministered at Ephesus until the reign of Trajan (ca. A.D. 98). The final composition of John's Gospel—including the epilogue (chapter 21)— could have taken place anywhere between A.D. 80 and 100. It could be that the initial work began even earlier, and then the final draft, complete with the appended epilogue, was finished later.

The Gospel of John was written fairly late in New Testament history, so its contents reveal different emphases from those of the synoptic Gospels. John was much more interested in explaining who Jesus *is* than what he did. This is made immediately evident by the prologue to the Gospel, which describes Jesus Christ as "the Word" who is God and who has been with God since the beginning of time (1:1). Furthermore, he is the unique Son of God, who is able to reveal the Father to humans (1:18). Throughout the rest of the book, Jesus carries out this role as he interacts with his disciples and argues with his opponents. Jesus' miracles are referred to as "signs" of greater truths, rather than as mere displays of divine power. The stories recounted by John are filled with symbolic and theological meaning, such as Jesus' repeated use of the phrase "I am" (4:26; 8:24; 13:19). This is the same name that God used for himself when he spoke to Moses in the Old Testament.

John wrote his Gospel to convince readers that "Jesus is the Messiah, the Son of God, and that by believing in him you will have life" (20:31). He made a special effort to encourage those who had come to believe in Jesus Christ, despite never having seen him (20:29). John's Gospel is probably the most universally appealing book in the New Testament. It brilliantly conveys developed theology through warmly intimate interactions and discussions with Jesus Christ.

The Prologue (1:1-18)
Jesus' First Disciples (1:19-51)
Jesus' Public Ministry: Seven Signs (2:1–12:51)
Jesus' Discourse in the Upper Room (13:1–17:26)
Jesus' Arrest, Trial, and Crucifixion (18:1–19:37)
Jesus' Burial and Resurrection (19:38–20:31)
The Epilogue (21:1-25)

. . . . .REVELATION

The Revelation (or "Apocalypse") of John is undoubtedly the most difficult and confusing book for most readers of the New Testament. The book is a combination of both epistle and apocalyptic prophecy. The first three chapters are written as letters to seven churches in Asia Minor. The rest of the book recounts a fantastic vision involving bizarre creatures, divine beings, symbolic signs and numbers, and various plagues and curses. At the end of this extraordinary vision, the faithful are rewarded, and the evil are condemned.

The author of this book is traditionally held to be the apostle John. The book itself identifies its author as John (1:1, 4, 9; 22:8) but does not specify which one. The earliest church writers state that John was exiled to Patmos under the emperor Domitian (ca. A.D. 90–95). It is here that John recorded his symbolic visions for the churches of Asia Minor. For many scholars, however, the content and style of Revelation seem so radically different from John's other writings that they find it difficult to believe these books were all written by the same author. Even the early church was divided over this issue. The Eastern church questioned John's authorship for centuries and so were slow to include Revelation in the canon. The Western church was less apprehensive and added the book to the canon much earlier.

Regardless of the author's identity, the purpose of the book remains clear: to encourage and exhort Christians who were undergoing persecution for their faith. By the time Revelation was being written, the church had been subjected to fierce persecution under both Nero and Domitian. Christians were harassed, evicted, tortured, and killed for believing in Jesus Christ, much like the Jews who were persecuted by the Seleucids and Antiochus Epiphanes centuries earlier. In order to give hope to these believers, John recorded his vision of ultimate redemption for the faithful.

The book of Revelation is replete with what has been termed "apocalyptic" imagery. Apocalypticism grew out of the Seleucid era when, as mentioned earlier, faithful Jews were persecuted for their religious beliefs. In reaction to this persecution, many came to view the world as being temporarily under the reign of the evil one. Ultimately, however, God would supernaturally enter history and restore everything. In the meantime, terrible ordeals and conflicts would occur as portents of the coming end. Many literary works were written from this perspective, and they tended to have similar literary features. These included vision stories, exotic creatures, divine beings, symbolic names and numbers, and cosmic conflicts between good and evil forces. Many extrabiblical works were written as apocalypses (meaning "uncoverings").

Revelation opens with a brief introduction, identifying the book as a prophecy given to John from Jesus Christ. Seven letters to seven churches in Asia Minor follow, citing various shortcomings and giving instruction and correction for their spiritual well-being. It is possible that the seven churches represent the entire church, rather than just the particular ones named, since the number seven was thought to represent completeness or wholeness. These seven letters establish several themes that are addressed later in the apocalyptic narrative section. This connects the body of the book with its beginning, giving a literary unity to the whole work.

The narrative then picks up with another sequence of apocalyptic visions intended to show John "what must happen after these things" (4:1). The imagery portrayed in these visions draws heavily from Old Testament prophecy and from such apocalyptic writings as 2 Esdras and 1 Enoch.

This section opens by ushering the reader into the throne room of God. In God's right hand is a seven-sealed scroll, which the Lamb, Jesus Christ, comes forward to open. As each of the seven seals are broken, various symbolic creatures and events are released. Then the angels of heaven blow seven trumpets, and the same sort of cycle takes place. After this, seven signs are given to represent different events and people. Seven bowls are poured out, unleashing terrible plagues and curses upon the earth. After all this, the fall of "Babylon" is recited, as well as the destruction of a terrible beast and a false prophet. Jesus Christ then returns to the earth to reign for a thousand years. After this era, Satan is released in order to rally his forces for a cataclysmic final battle with the forces of heaven. Satan is finally defeated, and those who sided with him are judged. God finally restores everything by creating a new heaven and a new earth. Revelation then draws to a close where the Old Testament opened—with a perfect world where the tree of life is watered by the freely flowing river of life. The vision ends with Jesus alerting the churches that he is indeed coming soon to fulfill all these things.

This fantastic book is almost certainly the most widely disputed as to its ultimate meaning. There seem to be as many interpretations of its symbolism as there are scholars to study it. Basically, however, there are three general schools of thought: (1) Almost the entire prophecy of Revelation refers to events of the first century;

(2) the prophecies delineate the history of the church from John's time to the end of the world; and (3) almost the entire prophecy refers to future events to be fulfilled immediately before Christ's second coming. Whatever view is taken, the presentation in the book itself is that the seven seals, trumpets, and bowls usher in Christ's return to the earth. At that time Christ will restore all things and reward the righteous. This reassuring thought for persecuted Christians is vividly communicated through the rich imagery of apocalyptic story. The book of Revelation provides a fitting end to the story of the New Testament.

Prologue (1:1-8)
Jesus among the Seven Churches (1:9-20)
The Letters to the Seven Churches (2:1–3:22)
The Throne, the Scroll, and the Lamb (4:1–5:14)
The Seven Seals (6:1–8:1)
The Seven Trumpets (8:2–11:19)
The Seven Signs (12:1–14:20)
The Seven Bowls (15:1–16:21)
The Destruction of Babylon (17:1–19:10)
The Destruction of the Beast and False Prophet (19:11-21)
The Thousand Years (20:1-6)
Satan's Judgment (20:7-10)
Great White Throne Judgment (20:11-15)
New Heaven, New Earth, New Jerusalem (21:1–22:5)
Epilogue (22:6-21)

SELECTED BIBLIOGRAPHY

The Synoptic Gospels

Aune, David E. *The New Testament in Its Literary Environment.* Vol. 8, Library of Early Christianity. Philadelphia: Westminster, 1987.

Caird, George B. *The Gospel of Saint Luke.* Westminster Pelican Series. Philadelphia: The Westminster Press, 1964.

Calvin, John. *Commentary on the Harmony of the Evangelists.* 1564. Reprint, Grand Rapids: Baker Book House, 1979.

Carson, D. A. "Matthew." In *The Expositor's Bible Commentary.* Vol. 8. Edited by F. E. Gaebelein. Grand Rapids: Zondervan, 1984.

Cole, A. *The Gospel according to Mark.* Tyndale New Testament Commentary. Grand Rapids: Eerdmans, 1961.

Conzelmann, Hans. *The Theology of Saint Luke.* New York: Harper & Row, 1960.

Cranfield, C. E. B. *The Gospel according to Saint Mark.* Cambridge: Cambridge University Press, 1959.

Ellison, H. L. "Matthew." In *The New Layman's Bible Commentary.* Glasgow: Pickering & Inglis, 1979.

Geldenhuys, Johannes. *Commentary on the Gospel of Luke.* New International Commentary. Grand Rapids: Eerdmans, 1951.

Hunter, A. M. "The Gospel according to Saint Mark." In *Torch Bible Commentary.* London: SCM, 1967.

Leaney, A. R. C. *A Commentary on the Gospel according to Saint Luke.* Harper's New Testament Commentaries. New York: Harper & Brothers, 1958.

Liefeld, Walter. "Luke." In *The Expositor's Bible Commentary.* Vol. 8. Edited by F. E. Gaebelein. Grand Rapids: Zondervan, 1984.

Lightfoot, Neil. *Parables of Jesus.* Grand Rapids: Baker Book House, 1963.

Manson, T. W. *The Sayings of Jesus.* London: SCM, 1949.

Marshall, I. Howard. *Luke: Historian and Theologian.* Grand Rapids: Zondervan, 1971.

Nineham, D. E. *Studies in the Gospels.* Naperville, Ill.: Allenson, 1955.

Nixon, R. E. "Matthew." In *The New Bible Commentary: Revised.* London: InterVarsity Press, 1970.

Schweizer, Eduard. *The Good News according to Mark.* London: SPCK, 1971.

Taylor, Vincent. *The Gospel according to Saint Mark*. London: Macmillan, 1952.

Tinsley, E. J. *Gospel according to Luke*. Cambridge Bible Commentary on the New English Bible. Cambridge: Cambridge University Press, 1965.

Trench, R. C. *Studies in the Gospels*. London: Macmillan, 1878.

Walvoord, John. *Matthew: Thy Kingdom Come*. Chicago: Moody, 1974.

Wessel, Walter. "Mark." In *The Expositor's Bible Commentary*. Vol. 8. Edited by F. E. Gaebelein. Grand Rapids: Zondervan, 1978.

John

Barrett, C. K. *The Gospel according to Saint John*. Philadelphia: The Westminster Press, 1978.

Bruce, F. F. *The Gospel of John*. Grand Rapids: Eerdmans, 1982.

Dods, Marcus. "The Gospel of Saint John." In *The Expositor's Greek Testament*. London: Hodder and Stoughton, 1899.

MacGregor, G. H. C. "The Gospel of John." In *The Moffat New Testament Commentary*. London: Hodder and Stoughton, Ltd., 1928.

Moberly, R. C. *Atonement and Personality*. London: John Murray, 1909.

Morris, Leon. *The Gospel according to John*. Grand Rapids: Eerdmans, 1971.

Pink, A. W. *Exposition of the Gospel of John*. Grand Rapids: Zondervan, 1973.

Titus, Eric L. *The Message of the Fourth Gospel*. Nashville: Abingdon Press, 1967.

Westcott, B. F. *The Gospel according to Saint John*. 1881. Reprint, Grand Rapids: Zondervan, 1973.

Acts

Bruce, F. F. *The Acts of the Apostles*. Chicago: InterVarsity Press, 1952.

Conybeare, W. J., and J. S. Howson. *The Life and Epistles of Saint Paul*. 1851. Reprint, Grand Rapids: Eerdmans, 1978.

Longenecker, Richard. "The Acts of the Apostles." In *The Expositor's Bible Commentary*. Vol. 9. Edited by F. E. Gaebelein. Grand Rapids: Zondervan, 1981.

Metzger, Bruce M. *The New Testament: Its Background, Growth, and Content*. 2d ed. Nashville: Abingdon Press, 1965, 1983.

The Letters of Paul to the Churches

Barrett, C. K. *A Commentary on the Epistle to the Romans*. New York: Harper & Brothers, 1957.

Berkhof, Hendrikus. *Doctrine of the Holy Spirit*. Atlanta: John Knox Press, 1976.

Boice, James M. "Galatians." In *The Expositor's Bible Commentary*. Vol. 10. Edited by F. E. Gaebelein. Grand Rapids: Zondervan, 1978.

Bruce, F. F. *The Epistle of Paul to the Romans* in the Tyndale New Testament Commentaries. Grand Rapids: Eerdmans, 1963.

————. "The Epistle to the Colossians, to Philemon, and to the Ephesians." In *The New International Commentary on the New Testament*. Grand Rapids: Eerdmans, 1984.

Brunner, Emil. *The Letter to the Romans, A Commentary*. London: Lutterworth, 1959.

Calvin, John. *Commentary on the Epistle of Paul the Apostle to the Romans*. 1583. Reprint, Grand Rapids: Eerdmans, 1947.

————. *Commentary on the Epistles of Paul the Apostle to the Corinthians*. 1577. Reprint, Edinburgh: Calvin Translation Society, 1848–49.

————. *The Epistles of Paul the Apostle to the Galatians, Ephesians, Philippians and Colossians*. 1546? Translated by T. H. L. Parker, and edited by David W. Torrance and Thomas F. Torrance. Grand Rapids: Eerdmans, 1965.

Constable, Thomas L. "First Thessalonians." In *The Bible Knowledge Commentary*. Wheaton, Ill.: Victor Books, 1983.

Cullman, Oscar. *The State in the New Testament*. New York: Scribner, 1956.

Davidson, F., and Ralph Martin. "Romans." In *The New Bible Commentary: Revised*. Edited by Guthrie and Motyer. London: InterVarsity Press, 1953, 1970.

Fee, Gordon. "The First Epistle to the Corinthians." In *The New International Commentary on the New Testament*. Grand Rapids: Eerdmans, 1987.

Findlay, G. G. "Saint Paul's First Epistle to the Corinthians." In *The Expositor's Greek Testament*. London: Hodder & Stoughton, 1917.

Gaffin, Richard. *The Centrality of the Resurrection*. Grand Rapids: Baker Book House, 1978.

Harris, Murray J. "Second Corinthians." In *The Expositor's Bible Commentary*. Vol. 10. Edited by F. E. Gaebelein. Grand Rapids: Zondervan, 1978.

Harrison, Everett. New Testament ed. *Wycliffe Bible Commentary*. Chicago: Moody Press, 1962.

Hawthorne, Gerald. *Philippians*. Vol. 43, Word Biblical Commentary. Waco: Word, 1983.

Hillyer, Norman. "First and Second Corinthians." In *The New Bible Commentary: Revised*. London: InterVarsity Press, 1970.

Kennedy, H. A. A. "Philippians." In *The Expositor's Greek Testament*. London: Hodder & Stoughton, 1917.

Kent, Homer. "Philippians." In *The Expositor's Bible Commentary*. Vol. 11. Edited by F. E. Gaebelein. Grand Rapids: Zondervan, 1978.

Lightfoot, J. B. *The Epistle of Saint Paul to the Galatians*. 1865. Reprint, Grand Rapids: Zondervan, 1957.

————. *Saint Paul's Epistles to the Colossians and to Philemon*. New York: Macmillan & Co., 1879.

————. *Saint Paul's Epistle to the Philippians*. New York: Macmillan & Co., 1868.

————. *Saint Paul's Epistle to the Romans*. London: Macmillan & Co., 1913.

Lightner, Robert. "Philippians." In *The Bible Knowledge Commentary*. Wheaton, Ill.: Victor Books, 1983.

Lincoln, Andrew T. *Ephesians*. Vol. 43, Word Biblical Commentary. Waco: Word, 1990.

Luther, Martin. *Commentary on the Epistle to the Romans*. 1522. Reprint, Grand Rapids: Zondervan, 1954.

————. *A Commentary on Saint Paul's Epistle to the Galatians*. 1535. Reprint, Westwood, N.J.: Fleming H. Revell, 1953.

Mare, W. Harold. "First Corinthians." In *The Expositor's Bible Commentary*. Vol. 10. Edited by F. E. Gaebelein. Grand Rapids: Zondervan, 1978.

Meeks, Wayne. *The First Urban Christians: The Social World of the Apostle Paul*. New Haven, Conn.: Yale University Press, 1984.

Rupprecht, Arthur A. "Philemon." In *The Expositor's Bible Commentary*. Vol. 11. Edited by F. E. Gaebelein. Grand Rapids: Zondervan, 1978.

Thomas, Robert L. "First Thessalonians." In *The Expositor's Bible Commentary*. Vol. 11. Edited by F. E. Gaebelein. Grand Rapids: Zondervan, 1978.

————. "Second Thessalonians." In *The Expositor's Bible Commentary*. Vol. 11. Edited by F. E. Gaebelein. Grand Rapids: Zondervan, 1978.

Vaughn, Curtis. "Colossians." In *The Expositor's Bible Commentary*. Vol. 11. Edited by F. E. Gaebelein. Grand Rapids: Zondervan, 1978.

The Pastoral Epistles

Auberlen, Karl. *The Epistles of Paul*. New York: Charles Scribners, 1870.

Calvin, John. *Commentaries on the Epistles to Timothy, Titus, and Philemon*. 1856. Reprint, Grand Rapids: Eerdmans, 1948.

Earle, Ralph. "First Timothy." In *The Expositor's Bible Commentary*. Vol. 11. Edited by F. E. Gaebelein. Grand Rapids: Zondervan, 1978.

————. "Second Timothy." In *The Expositor's Bible Commentary*. Vol. 11. Edited by F. E. Gaebelein. Grand Rapids: Zondervan, 1978.

Hiebert, D. Edmond. *First Timothy*. Chicago: Moody Press, 1967.

White, Newport J. D. "First and Second Epistles to Timothy." In *The Expositor's Greek Testament*. Grand Rapids: Eerdmans, 1979.

The General Epistles

Bauckham, Richard J. *Jude, 2 Peter*. Vol. 50, Word Biblical Commentary. Waco: Word, 1983.

Blum, Edwin A. "Jude." In *The Expositor's Bible Commentary*. Vol. 12. Edited by F. E. Gaebelein. Grand Rapids: Zondervan, 1981.

———. "First Peter." In *The Expositor's Bible Commentary*. Vol. 12. Edited by F. E. Gaebelein. Grand Rapids: Zondervan, 1981.

———. "Second Peter." In *The Expositor's Bible Commentary*. Vol. 12. Edited by F. E. Gaebelein. Grand Rapids: Zondervan, 1981.

Bruce, F. F. *The Epistles of John: Introduction, Exposition, Notes*. Grand Rapids: Eerdmans, 1970.

Burdick, Donald W. "James." In *The Expositor's Bible Commentary*. Vol. 12. Edited by F. E. Gaebelein. Grand Rapids: Zondervan, 1981.

Calvin, John. *The Epistles of Paul the Apostle to the Hebrews and the First and Second Epistles of Saint Peter*. Edinburgh: Oliver & Boyd, 1963.

Hawthorne, Gerald F. "The Letter to the Hebrews." In *Bible Commentary for Today*. Glasgow: Pickering & Inglis, 1979.

Kelly, J. N. D. *A Commentary on the Epistles of Peter and Jude*. The Harper New Testament Commentaries. New York: Harper & Row, 1969.

Luther, Martin. *The Epistles of Saint Peter and Saint Jude*. c. 1530. Translated 1904. Reprint, Grand Rapids: Kregel, 1982.

———. "Lectures on the First Epistle of Saint John." In *Luther's Works*. Vol. 30. Translated by W. A. Hansen. St. Louis: Concordia Publishing House, 1967.

Marshall, I. H. "The Epistles of John." In *The New International Commentary*. Grand Rapids: Eerdmans, 1978.

Mayor, J. B. "The Epistle of Jude." In *The Expositor's Greek Testament*. Grand Rapids: Eerdmans, 1979.

Morris, Leon. "Hebrews." In *The Expositor's Bible Commentary*. Vol. 12. Edited by F. E. Gaebelein. Grand Rapids: Zondervan, 1981.

Smith, David. "First John." In *The Expositor's Greek Testament*. Grand Rapids: Eerdmans, 1979.

Vine, W. E. *The Epistles of John: Light, Love, Life*. Grand Rapids: Zondervan, 1970 (by permission of Oliphants).

Westcott, B. F. *The Epistle to the Hebrews*. London: Macmillan & Co., 1892.

Revelation

Auberlen, Karl. *The Prophecies of Daniel and the Revelations of Saint John, Viewed in Their Mutual Relation*. Edinburgh: T & T Clark, 1856.

Beasley-Murray, G. R. "The Revelation." In *The New Bible Commentary: Revised*. Grand Rapids: Eerdmans, 1970.

Bruce, F. F. "The Revelation to John." In *A New Testament Commentary*. Grand Rapids: Zondervan, 1969.

Bullinger, E. W. *Commentary on Revelation*. 1935. Reprint, Grand Rapids: Kregel, 1984.

Caird, G. B. *The Revelation of Saint John the Divine*. The Harper New Testament Commentaries. New York: Harper & Row, 1966.

Charles, R. H. *A Critical and Exegetical Commentary on the Revelation of Saint John*. 2 vols. The International Critical Commentary series. Edinburgh: T & T Clark, 1920.

Hendriksen, William. *More than Conquerors; an Interpretation of the Book of Revelation*. Grand Rapids: Baker Book House, 1967.

Johnson, Alan F. "Revelation." In *The Expositor's Bible Commentary*. Vol. 12. Edited by F. E. Gaebelein. Grand Rapids: Zondervan, 1981.

Ladd, George E. *A Commentary on the Revelation of John*. Grand Rapids: Eerdmans, 1972.

Larkin, Clarence. *The Book of Revelation*. Glenside, Pa.: Clarence Larkin Estate, n.d.

McDowell, Edward A. *The Meaning and Message of the Book of Revelation*. Nashville: Broadman Press, 1951.

Pieters, Albertus. *Studies in the Revelation of Saint John*. Grand Rapids: Eerdmans, 1954.

Ramsay, William M. *The Letters to the Seven Churches of Asia*. London: Hodder & Stoughton, 1904.

Seiss, Joseph A. *Apocalypse*. Grand Rapids: Zondervan, n.d.

Summers, R. *Worthy Is the Lamb*. Nashville: Broadman, 1951.

Swete, Henry Barclay. *The Apocalypse of Saint John*. New York: Macmillan & Co., 1906.

Talbot, Louis. *The Revelation of Jesus Christ*. 1937. Reprint, Grand Rapids: Eerdmans, 1973.

Torrance, Thomas F. *Apocalypse Today*. Greenwood, S.C.: Attic Press, 1960.

Trench, Richard C. *Commentary on the Epistle to the Seven Churches*. Reprint, Minneapolis: Klock & Klock, 1978.

Walvoord, John F. *The Revelation of Jesus Christ*. Chicago: Moody Press, 1966.